COLLECTIVE BARGAINING AND GENDER EQUALITY

The Gendered Economy

Series Editors: Sara Cantillon and Diane Elson

This path-breaking new series critically examines the economy and the theory and methodology of economics through the lens of gender. It will publish original and incisive research that explores the role of gender in the contemporary global economy. The series showcases how economic relationships, actions and institutions are directly affected by gender norms, how a gendered perspective illuminates aspects of the economy that would otherwise be ignored, and challenges many of the tenets that underpin both the mainstream and heterodox interpretation of how economies function.

Published

Collective Bargaining and Gender Equality
Jane Pillinger and Nora Wintour

The Economy's Other Half
James Heintz

The Sex Economy
Monica O'Connor

COLLECTIVE BARGAINING AND GENDER EQUALITY

Jane Pillinger
and
Nora Wintour

agenda
publishing

We dedicate this book to our sisters

First published in 2019 by Agenda Publishing

Agenda Publishing Limited
The Core
Bath Lane
Newcastle Helix
Newcastle upon Tyne
NE4 5TF
www.agendapub.com

ISBN 978-1-78821-076-8

British Library Cataloguing-in-Publication Data
A catalogue record for this book is available from the British Library

Typeset by JS Typesetting Ltd, Porthcawl, Mid Glamorgan
Printed and bound in the UK by Short Run Press Ltd, Exeter, Devon

Contents

Acknowledgements

We want to thank the many women and men we have worked with over the years in national and global unions, in social dialogue structures and in the ILO, whose work and dedication to gender equality have provided much of the inspiration for us in writing this book. Thanks also go to our editor at Agenda, Alison Howson, who gave much appreciated advice and suggestions during the writing of the book; to Steven Gerrard for guidance and support during the publishing process; and to Tomáš Žák for his great help with the index.

Acronyms

3F Denmark	United Federation of Danish Workers
ACTU	Australian Council of Trade Unions
AEU	Australian Education Union
AFL-CIO	American Federation of Labor and Congress of Industrial Organizations
AIBTMF	All India Brick and Tiles Manufacturing Federation
ANCI	Associazione Nazionale Comuni Italiani [National Association of Italian Communes]
ANEF	Agrupación Nacional de Empleados Fiscales [National Association of Tax Employees of Chile]
BAO	Employers' Association of the Swedish Banking Institutions
BFAWU	Bakers, Food and Allied Workers Union, UK
BWI	Building and Woodworkers' International
CARVE	Companies Against Gender Violence EU
CBA	collective bargaining agreement
CCOO	Comisiones Obreras [Workers' Commission, Spain]
CEACR	ILO Committee of Experts on the Application of Conventions and Recommendations
CEASE Europe	European Corporate Network – involving companies to cease gender-based violence project
CEDAW	UN Convention on the Elimination of All Forms of Discrimination Against Women
CEEP Europe	European Centre of Employers and Enterprises providing Public Services and Services of general interest

CEMR	Council of European Municipalities and Regions
CGIL	Confederazione Generale Italiana del Lavoro [General Confederation of Labour, Italy]
CISL	Confederazione Italiana Sindacati Lavoratori [Italian Confederation of Workers' Trade Unions]
CLC	Canadian Labour Congress
CMKOS	Czech-Moravian Confederation of Trade Unions
CNE	Centrale national des employés [National Workers' Centre, Belgium]
CoESS	Confédération européenne des services de sécurité [European Confederation of Security Services]
COLSIBA	Coordinadora Latinomericana de Sindicatos Bananeros y Agroindustriales [Coordinating Body of Latin American Banana and Agro-Industrial Unions]
CONADU	Federación Nacional de Docentes Universitarios [National Federation of University Teachers, Argentina]
COSATU	Congress of South African Trade Unions
CoP	Community of Practice
CREVAWC	Centre for Research and Education on Violence Against Women and Children, Canada
CSC Belgium	Confédération des syndicats chrétiens [Confederation of Christian Trade Unions, Belgium]
CUPE	Canadian Union of Public Employees
CUT Brazil	Central Única dos Trabalhadores [United Workers' Central]
CUT Chile	Central Unitaria de Trabajadores de Chile [Workers' United Center of Chile]
ECJ	European Court of Justice
EDF	Électricté de France [Electricity of France]
EFEE	European Federation of Education Employers
EI	Education International
EIS	The Educational Institute of Scotland
ENEL	Ente nazionale per l'energia elettrica [National Electricity Board, Italy]

EPSEL S.A.	Entidad Prestadora de Servicio de Saneamiento de Lambayeque [Sanitation Services Enterprise of Lambayeque, Peru]
EPSU	European Public Service Union
ESF	European Structural Fund
ETF	European Transport Federation
ETUC	European Trade Union Confederation
ETUCE	European Trade Union Committee for Education
ETUI	European Trade Union Institute
EPZ	export processing zone
EWC	European Works Council
FENTAP	Federación de Trabajadores del Agua Potable y Alcantarillado del Perú [Federation of Workers of Drinking Water and Sewage Systems of Peru]
FILTCEM	Federazione Italiana Lavoratori Chimica Tessile Energia Manifatture [Italian Federation of Chemical, Textiles, Energy and Manufacturing Workers]
FLAEI	Federazione Lavoratori Aziende Elettriche Italiane [Italian Federation of Electricity Company Workers]
FO	Force Ouvrière [Workers' Force, France]
FMLA	Family and Medical Leave Act
FSU	Finansförbundet [Financial Sector Union of Sweden]
GDF	Gaz de France [Gas of France]
GFA	global framework agreement
GMB	originally General Municipal Boilermakers
GPA-djp	Gewerkschaft der Privatangestellten, Druck, Journalismus, Papier [Union of Private Sector Employees, Printing, Journalism and Paper]
GPMU	Graphical, Paper and Media Union
GRPS	gender-responsive public services
GTUC	Ghana Trade Union Congress
GUF	Global Union Federation
HRCT Nordic	Nordic Hotel, Restaurant, Catering and Tourism Union

HK-Denmark	Handels-og Kontorfunktionærernes Forbund [Commerce and Office Workers Union of Denmark]
HNSA	HomeNet South Asia
HOSPEEM	European Hospital and Healthcare Employers' Association
IG-Metall	Industriegewerkschaft Metall [Metalworkers' Union, Germany]
ICFTU	International Confederation of Free Trade Unions
IDWF	International Domestic Workers Federation
ILO	International Labour Organization
ITF	International Transport Federation
ITGWLF	International Textile, Garment, Leather Workers Federation
ITUC	International Trade Union Confederation
IFC	International Finance Corporation
IUF	International Union of Food, Agriculture, Hotel, Restaurant, Catering, Tobacco and Allied Workers' Associations
KTO Denmark	Kommunale Tjenestemænd og Overskomstansatte [Association of Local Government Employees' Organizations]
KUDHEIHA	Kenya Union of Domestic, Hotels, Educational Institutions, Hospitals and Allied Workers
LO-Sweden	Landsorganisationen i Sverige [National Organization, Sweden]
MNCR	Movimento Nacional dos Catadores de Materais Recicláveis [National Movement of Waste Pickers, Brazil]
MNE	multinational enterprise
NASVI	National Alliance of Street Vendors of India
NHS	National Health Service, UK
NTEU	National Tertiary Education Union, Australia
NUS	National Union of Students, UK
OECD	Organization for Economic Cooperation and Development

ÖGB	Österreichischer Gewerkschaftsbund [Austrian Trade Union Federation]
PIT-CNT	Plenario Intersindical de Trabajadores-Convención Nacional de Trabajadores [Plenary of Workers' Unions – National Convention of Workers]
PRO-GE	Die Produkutions Gewerkschaft [Manufacturing Trade Union, Austria]
PCS	Public and Commercial Services Union
PSA	Public Service Association Te Pūkenga Here Tikanga Mahi, New Zealand
PSI	Public Services International
SACCAWU	South African Commercial, Catering and Allied Workers Union
SACO	Sveriges Akademiker [Swedish Confederation of Professional Associations]
SEWA	Self-employed Women's Association, India
SSSS	single spine salary system
STUC	Scottish Trades Union Congress
SUTD	Sindicato Único de Trabajadoras Domesticas [Trade Union of Domestic Workers, Uruguay]
TUC	Trades Union Congress, UK
TUCA	Trade Union Confederation of the Americas
UATGWU	Ugandan Amalgamated Transport and General Workers Union
UBI	universal basic income
UCU	University and College Union, UK
UEAPME	European Association of Craft, Small and Medium-sized Enterprises
UNCSW	United National Commission on the Status of Women
UNI	Union Network International
UNITE	Unite – the Union, UK
UNISON	UNISON – the public service union, UK
UIL	Unione Italiana del Lavoro [Italian Labour Union]
UILTEC	Unione Italiana Lavoratori Tessile Energia Chimica [Italian Union of Textile, Energy and Chemical Workers]

UPI	Unione Province d'Italia [Union of Italian Provinces]
UPTA	Unión de Profesionales y Trabajadores Autónomos [Union of Professional Autonomous Workers, Spain]
USDAW	Union of Shop, Distributive and Allied Workers, UK
Vida	Gerwerkshaft Vida [Austrian Public Services Union]
WIEGO	Women in Informal Employment Globalizing and Organizing

Foreword

Sara Cantillon and Diane Elson

The Gendered Economy is a new path-breaking series of short books which critically examine our understanding of the economy through the lens of gender and expose the androcentric biases within mainstream and heterodox economic analysis.

This book contributes to the series by looking how trade unions and other membership-based workers' organizations can support gender equality, drawing on examples from across the world. This issue is missing from most of the global reports on women's economic empowerment, from organizations like the World Bank and the IMF, which celebrate individual entrepreneurship but ignore collective action. As more women take up paid employment, they are joining trade unions or other membership-based organizations in growing numbers, so that in some countries women now outnumber men in trade unions. But this book is clear-eyed about the challenges: collective agreements often cover only male dominated industries and the public sector, and usually have not included sub-contracted workers; trade unions have often been slow to take up gender equality issues; and the majority of women in employment in many countries are in the informal economy where organizing is much more difficult.

Nevertheless, as this book shows, change is happening. Collective bargaining agendas have been broadened to address issues such as workplace discrimination, equal pay for work of equal value, the care responsibilities of workers, and the impact of domestic violence in the workplace. Women are increasingly participating in the leadership of some trade unions.

This book does not only look at traditional trade union organizing. It also looks at new ways of organizing workers in informal employment, and the ways in which trade unions can support this in networks developed with NGOs, and in bargaining forums in which trade unions participate alongside informal workers' organizations. Global Framework Agreements have established new bargaining frameworks at transnational level, and some have sought to cover sub-contracted workers throughout the supply chain. Trade unions have participated in multi-stakeholder initiatives, such as the Ethical Trading Initiative. Some trade unions have also begun to engage with the communities who use the services they produce. For example, teachers' unions have engaged with parents in campaigns for good quality public education; while health care unions have focused on the quality of patient care.

This book concludes that a broader perspective beyond the immediate workplace, focusing on citizen's rights as well as labour rights, and including concern with the impact of spending on public services and on taxation is critical for strengthening the impact of collective bargaining on gender equality in the future.

Introduction

This book examines the role and contribution of collective bargaining to gender equality in the context of globalization and women's struggles, organizing and advocacy in trade unions. It tracks how union collective bargaining agendas have shifted to reflect women's struggles for equality, providing avenues for sustainable gender equality gains. Building on the existing understanding of the role that women in trade unions have played in developing new agendas for "equality bargaining", it reviews recent collective bargaining breakthroughs in areas such as equal pay, work–life balance and gender-based violence in the world of work. While the focus is mainly on European countries, initiatives related to union organizing and negotiating for women workers in developing country contexts and through global supply chains are integrated throughout the book, reflecting increased attention to this work over the past two decades. Nonetheless, it remains true that the vast majority of women, whether in paid employment, self-employment or informal work, do not benefit from collective bargaining coverage, particularly in the global south and in fragile states.

The authors draw on over three decades of engagement on equality issues with trade unions across the world. Based on primary evidence, original research and surveys, as well as the authors' own participation in global union campaigns on issues such as pay equity, maternity protection, organizing self-employed and informal women workers, on migrant workers and on gender-based violence, the book also includes insights gained as a result of engagement with recent national, European and global social dialogue initiatives.

Despite the many challenges, it is important to recall that trade unions are the largest collective organization of women across the world. Collective bargaining remains critically important in the globalized economy, precisely because of new employment patterns and the increasing incidence of precarious work. By pointing to recent promising developments in collective bargaining, the book also reflects on some ways forward for collective bargaining to play a more central role in achieving gender equality.

UNION CONTRADICTIONS AND CHALLENGES IN RELATION TO GENDER EQUALITY

Trade unions were formed in the late nineteenth century to protect the interests of skilled male craft workers, a role later extended to the predominantly male workforce in manufacturing, transport and the public sector, mainly in Europe and North America. In this context, employment was based on an economic and social model of the family wage, women's dependence on men and the limited participation of women in paid work outside the home. Trade-union structures and bargaining agendas reflected this reality. However, in recent decades, as women entered the workforce in large numbers and joined trade unions – most recently at a faster pace than men – new issues, such as the undervaluing of women's work and women's unpaid care work have been brought into the public domain and onto trade union agendas.

Unions face both contradictions and challenges in relation to gender equality. Trade unions are significant societal institutions, whose formation, roles and activities have been shaped by decades of male dominance and unequal gender roles and relations. Forms of representation and organizing have been slow to change since male power structures and resistance have been hard to challenge. However, with the decline of male jobs in manufacturing and the rise of service industries in developed economies, and particularly women's employment in the public services, trade unions have adapted to the increasing feminization of work and rising female membership. Within trade unions themselves, the focus has been on women's participation in decision-making and challenges to traditional methods of bargaining in a patriarchal system, described by the South African trade union COSATU (2016) as "a struggle within the struggle".

Unions can give voice to and channel women's workplace concerns into collective bargaining. As one UK trade unionist recently said:

> When your black and women members see union reps who are like them and they see that they can do something to protect their rights, then they think that the union is relevant to them and they will join unions. That's why we are seeing such a positive change in the union movement now.[1]

Over the last two decades, despite the overall decline in union membership, the proportion of women's members has increased. In 2012, women comprised the majority of trade union members in a third of the 39 developing and developed countries for which data exists. In 16 countries, women comprised more than 40 per cent of total union membership (Cobble 2012). In Europe, women comprise around 45 per cent of union membership and there is a trend to reach gender parity in decision-making (ETUC 2017b). In the UK, union membership among women is now higher than it is for men; 55 per cent of union members were female in 2015, compared to 45 per cent in 1995 (Department for Business, Innovation & Skills 2015). A higher level of union membership and leadership positions amongst women exists in the Nordic and Baltic countries, than in other European countries.

Trade unions have become more relevant to women, as reflected in the expanded scope of collective bargaining on gender equality issues (Baird, McFerron & Wright 2014; Briskin 2006). In the UK, struggles to transform trade unions from male-dominated organizations into women-friendly organizations took place, particularly in the public sector, in the context of the combination of the "second wave" of feminism

---

1. Zita Holbourne, PCS National Vice President and Chair of the PCS Women's Committee, interviewed by Jane Pillinger.

and the introduction of gender equality legislation (Colgan & Ledwith 1996). In other countries, as is the case in Sri Lanka, women workers have challenged entrenched social norms and cultures that perpetuate the gendered division of labour and inequalities in trade unions (Withers & Biyanwila 2014). Global unions have also played a significant role in shaping equality agendas and supporting national trade unions in developing countries to address women's participation in trade union decision making and key workplace issues such as maternity protection, equal pay, living wages, gender-based violence and organizing informal, domestic and migrant workers.

Women's struggles in unions have brought new issues onto bargaining agendas, including the multiple and intersecting forms of discrimination faced by women, particularly working-class, black, migrant, LGBTI and other groups of marginalized women. In many contexts, traditional "male" bargaining agendas have been transformed, as is increasingly evident in the public sector, not only in Europe and North America but also in some African, Asian and Latin American countries. Furthermore, women in unions have used established occupational health and safety initiatives as an entry point to challenge patriarchy and unequal gender relations, by tackling issues such as women's safety and gender-based violence at work.

SOCIAL DIALOGUE, COLLECTIVE BARGAINING AND THE PROMOTION OF GENDER EQUALITY

The fundamental labour rights, as laid down in ILO Convention 87 on Freedom of Association and Protection of the Right to Organize (1948) and ILO Convention 98 on the Right to Organize and Collective Bargaining (1949) provide the normative framework for trade unions to represent workers and negotiate on their behalf. Many workers in countries across the world, particularly in developing countries, are denied the fundamental right to freedom of association, including the right to form and join a trade union and negotiate collective agreements. This situation is particularly true for the most marginalized workers at the lower end of global supply chains: informal workers, migrant workers, domestic workers and others.

In some countries collective bargaining remains very limited. In central and eastern Europe, collective bargaining exists principally at company level. This situation differs from the gradual shift of bargaining away from sectoral level to company level, that has taken place for example in Germany and the UK over the last two decades. In many developing countries, strong, independent unions are largely absent outside the public sector and larger private enterprises, while the great majority of workers are in precarious and informal work.

Collective bargaining is one aspect of the broader concept referred to by the International Labour Organization (ILO) as social dialogue. Social dialogue involves workers, employers and governments in decision-making on employment and work-related issues and "is both a means to achieve social and economic progress and an objective in itself, as it gives people a voice and stake in their societies and workplaces" (ILO 2013a: 5).

Social dialogue includes collective bargaining, and other forms of negotiation, cooperation and dispute resolution. Social dialogue can be bipartite between workers and employers, referred to as the social partners, or tripartite between government, workers and employers. Tripartite social dialogue includes consultations and discussions about public policies and laws affecting workers and employers. Collective bargaining is the means through which employers and their organizations and workers, organized in trade unions, negotiate wages and working conditions. The objective of these negotiations is to arrive at collective agreements that regulate terms and conditions of employment. Collective agreements also address the rights and responsibilities of both employers and trade unions.

Trade unions benefit all workers in unionized and non-unionized employment, in securing rights at work, fair pay, entitlements to holiday and sick leave, occupational safety and health and other protections in the workplace (ILO 2017a; Mishel & Walters 2003; Oxfam 2018; Schafer & Gottschall 2015). However, it is when women are present in union decision-making and in collective bargaining that there can be a notable difference in the attention given to promoting equality (Colgan & Ledwith 1996; Dickens 2000; ETUC 2010; Pillinger 2014).

Chapter 2 examines the preconditions and enablers for collective bargaining to contribute to gender equality, recognizing that a range of interlinking social and economic factors, women's advocacy, and progressive legislation all have a role to play. Strong trade unions and centralized or national-level collective bargaining have played a decisive role in promoting policies that benefit women and families, such as work–life balance and flexible working hours. In this context, collective bargaining has the *potential* to go further and be a crucial tool, among others, for achieving gender equality commitments in the UN's 2030 Sustainable Development Agenda (Goal 5: Achieve gender equality and empower all women and girls; and Goal 8: Promote inclusive and sustainable economic growth, employment and decent work for all, the latter of which includes social dialogue).

However, because bargaining has traditionally been stronger in male-dominated sectors (Schäfer & Gottschall 2015), collective bargaining can reinforce existing gender divisions and prevent the achievement of substantive equality (Briskin 2014a, 2014b; Guillaume 2013; Ledwith 2012). Traditional male bargaining models, as Dickens (2000) argues, continue to pose significant challenges for trade unions. Male resistance in trade unions (Cockburn 1991) has in the past often thwarted the campaigning and bargaining efforts of women, which is still evident today in many unions across the world.

Subsequent chapters examine how unions have adopted programmes of renewal, leading to changing gender power dynamics within unions and new organizing strategies and union agendas. Changing the structure of power relations in any large organization is a long-term objective: the challenge faced by unions is how to change these power dynamics from within (internal trade union policies and representation) and how to effect wider economic and social change (external influencing of the law and policy). These dynamics are discussed in Chapter 3 in relation to collective bargaining in three distinct areas: equal pay for work of equal value, work–life balance, and gender-based violence at work to showcase the transformations in bargaining in recent years.

COLLECTIVE BARGAINING AND NEW FORMS OF
EMPLOYMENT IN THE GLOBALIZED ECONOMY

The UN Special Rapporteur on the rights to freedom of peaceful assembly and of association considers that women and other groups face the most severe forms of discrimination and lack of rights:

> Women in the global economy are often relegated to low-paying, low-skills jobs. Persistent gender-based violence suppresses the individual and collective assertion of their rights to resist exploitative/abusive employers or State authorities. Further, certain groups of workers – including women; internal and external migrants; racial, ethnic, religious and sexual minorities; dispossessed rural workers and others – are often disenfranchised from the start by their status, making it more difficult to assert rights. (UN General Assembly 2016: 6)

Chapter 4 examines the issues and challenges relating to bargaining strategies to protect the rights of precarious workers and informal workers. In many countries, collective bargaining coverage has been seriously eroded in recent years (Visser, Hayter & Gammarano 2015). Particularly since the global economic crisis, there has been a weakening of collective bargaining mechanisms as a result of labour law deregulation and austerity policies that undermine the capacity of unions to bargain collectively. Overall union density has reduced and brought new forms of precarious employment, including in the so-called "gig" economy (Akhtar & Moore 2017; Heeks 2017; ILO 2016a; Johnston & Land-Kazlauskas 2018; Moore 2018). The new "precariat" (Standing 2011) is a "distinct social group" in insecure work denied basic civil, political, cultural, social and economic rights, and alienated from identification as members of the working class. In the UK, the TUC (2017) estimated that the growth of insecure and precarious jobs accounts for a 4.2 per cent decline in trade union membership in the previous year, where one in ten UK workers are now in precarious jobs.

While in some cases globalization has brought new employment opportunities for women in developed and developing countries, it has also created new loci for discrimination and exploitation, reinforcing and in some cases widening existing gender segmentation in the labour market. In India, for example, this is connected with service provision to the developed world through information technology enabled services (ITES) and business process outsourcing, such as call centres, and in the healthcare and hospitality sectors. These are also sectors and countries that have low levels of unionization and collective bargaining (ITUC 2017). In garment-producing countries, such as India, Bangladesh, Vietnam, Cambodia, Indonesia and Myanmar, factory employment provides an entry point for poor women, often young migrants from rural areas, into formal work, but it is work that is often exploitative and dangerous, and trade union representation is weak.

Globalization also brings new challenges to traditional bargaining models because they are based on national industrial relations frameworks, while a transnational response is now required. With the growth of multinational enterprises (MNEs), new global framework agreements have been negotiated. In some cases, they have been used to expose gross abuses of women's rights, for example, in export-orientated horticulture, garments and electronics (Asia Floor Wage Alliance *et al.* 2018; ILO 2016a; Morris & Pillinger 2016; Rosenbaum & Silliman 2018). These issues are explored in Chapter 5, with a particular focus on gender equality concerns across global supply chains and in export processing zones (EPZs) in developing countries.

2

The gender dimensions of collective bargaining

This chapter reviews the necessary preconditions for collective bargaining to promote gender equality. There is wide agreement that centralized (national or sector-wide) arrangements, strong employers' and workers' organizations, participation of women in negotiations, and government support for collective bargaining and equality are among the most important preconditions for gender equality to be progressed through collective bargaining (Dickens 1998; Hayter 2015; Rubery & Koukiadaki 2016). This chapter builds on this perspective by looking at seven inter-related preconditions that underpin gender equality dimensions of collective bargaining. These are set out in Figure 2.1 below. They relate to issues both inside and outside of the workplace.

1. STRONG SOCIAL DIALOGUE STRUCTURES

Level of bargaining and gender equality outcomes

Overall, collective bargaining on gender equality is more effective when national and sectoral bargaining lead to institutionalized forms of bargaining and wage setting (Hayter & Weinberg 2011; Rubery & Koukiadaki 2016). In a study of 19 countries where sectoral or national bargaining exists, over 75 per cent of wage earners were covered by collective bargaining agreements (CBAs) (Visser, Hayter & Gammarano 2015). In several countries in Europe (Austria, Germany and Belgium) and in South Africa, Brazil and Argentina, national and sectoral CBAs

Figure 2.1 Preconditions for collective bargaining to promote gender equality]

have reduced wage inequalities and contributed to productivity and competitiveness (Hayter 2012).

Gender differences are lower when bargaining is centralized and where there is a framework for equality, including model agreements implemented at the workplace (Heery 2006; Pillinger 2014; Ponzellini Aumayr & Wolf 2010). In countries with high levels of collective bargaining coverage, particularly where the law places obligations on companies to conclude collective agreements, and where there are national or sectoral agreements, less equality and smaller pay gaps are found, compared to countries with low bargaining coverage (Eurofound 2010; Hayter & Weinberg 2011; ILO 2011). In this regard Reegård argues that "coordinated wage bargaining from the centre reduces wage disparity and contributes to a more equal society" (2013: 114). Estimates suggest that with one per cent increase in social dialogue "coverage" the gender pay gap is reduced by 0.16 per cent (European Commission 2009) and the higher the degree of coordination in wage formation, the more equal the distribution of pay (ETUC 2012, 2013a; Tilly 2013). A survey by the UK's Department for Business, Innovation and Skills (2015) showed that the union wage premium – the gap between the hourly earnings of union members and non-members – was 16 per cent in the public sector and 7 per cent in the private sector. Data analyzed by the US National Women's Law Centre (2014) shows that the wage gap among union members in the USA is half the size of the wage gap among non-union workers. Female union members earn over $200 per week more than women who are not represented by unions, showing a significantly higher union premium for women than men.

National sectoral-level bargaining is the most effective way in which agenda setting on gender equality can be established across the economy or across a sector. Company-level bargaining can also play an important role in setting equality objectives, particularly if principles and targets are established either in legislation or in national sectoral agreements, for example, for the negotiation of workplace pay audits or surveys to detect the gender pay gap. Certain gender equality issues benefit from local agreements and local implementation, for example, flexible work for parents and negotiating leave for victims of domestic violence.

The greatest potential for gender equality outcomes is where these two levels coexist, as has been the case in France; although legal obligations for mainstreaming gender equality in workplace bargaining in French companies has been poorly monitored and enforced by the state (Milner & Gregory 2014). The general shift from sectoral bargaining towards company-level bargaining has led to greater fragmentation of bargaining in some countries, where outcomes are often reliant on local bargaining teams to identify priorities and actions, which may previously have been set in a systematic way at the sectoral level. Even in situations where collective bargaining exists, for example, through statutory bipartite workplace institutions, gender issues often have a very low priority in local collective bargaining (Sankaran & Madhav 2011). Therefore, a combination of central (sectoral or cross-sectoral) agreements that set out equality principles and frameworks, and company-level bargaining on issues such as workplace pay audits/surveys, flexible working time and reconciliation of work and family life, prove to be the most effective way to ensure equality outcomes across the economy.

Multi-employer bargaining

Multi-employer bargaining – where collective agreements are extended to all workers regardless of whether they are members of a union or not – offers protection for women in non-unionized and precarious employment, including migrant workers and women in small companies. A good example is from Norway where the Basic Agreement 2014–17 between the LO union confederation and the Confederation of Norwegian Enterprises sets out objectives that are contained in Part 1 of all collective agreements for the whole economy. A supplementary agreement on equality, the framework agreement on equality of life between women and men in working life, ensures multi-employer bargaining coverage for all women workers in all workplaces.

Collective bargaining coverage

Broad collective bargaining coverage is self-evidently an important precondition if gender equality is to be integrated into collective bargaining. There are wide variations in collective bargaining coverage across the world. Across 75 developed and developing countries, Visser, Hayter and Gammarano (2015) found that between 2005 and 2015, trade-union membership as a proportion of all employees, referred to as trade-union density, fell steadily in many parts of the world. However, it remained stable in some countries and increased in a few, for example, Chile, Denmark, Norway and Uruguay. Despite declining union membership in Europe, many countries have collective bargaining provisions that automatically extend rights to the whole workforce, whether they are in unionized workplaces or not.

Collective bargaining coverage ranged from one or two per cent of employees (not including self-employed or informal workers) in the Philippines and Peru to over 95 per cent coverage in France, Belgium, Uruguay and Finland. In most countries in Europe, there are few differences in collective bargaining coverage of male and female workers, and in some countries, such as Finland, Luxembourg, Canada and the UK, women actually enjoy higher levels of coverage than their male counterparts, particularly in the public sector. In Europe on average six out of ten workers are covered by CBAs that set wages (Eurofound 2014b). In Canada, there was a slight increase in the unionization rate in the public sector over the period 1981–2014 and women's unionization rates were relatively stable. In 2004, for the first time, the unionization rate for women at 31 per cent was slightly higher than for men (30%) and by 2012, women comprised half of all union members in Canada (Statistics Canada 2014).

The economic crisis had a profound impact on collective bargaining coverage, which fell by 4.6 per cent in 48 countries (Visser, Hayter & Gammarano 2015). This intensified the general trend towards more individualized, decentralized and fragmented bargaining, particularly evident in Europe (Briskin 2014b; ETUC 2013a, 2013b, 2017b; Eurofound 2015b; Pillinger 2014). The ten European countries most affected by the crisis saw collective bargaining coverage fall by an average of 21 per cent during the crisis (European Commission 2014a). The economic crisis further exacerbated women's employment insecurity, with fewer working hours, involuntary part-time work and occupational segregation, which were neglected in assessments of the crisis in Europe (Advisory Committee on Equal Opportunities for Women and Men 2009; ETUC 2011a, 2012a; Maier 2011). There was also a noticeable reduction in priority given to women's issues and a bias towards male-dominated rather than female-dominated sectors, for example, in national reform programmes (ETUC 2012a; Jepsen & Leschke 2011). In 2017 the European Trade Union Confederation (ETUC) began a campaign "Europe needs a pay rise" to ensure that the recovery included pay rises for all workers, with a particular emphasis on low-paid workers, and in 2018 the ETUC issued a call to action for governments to improve collective bargaining as a basis of reducing growing inequalities and precarious work. As the ETUC's Confederal Secretary, Esther Lynch argues, "revitalizing collective bargaining will make more people better off and strengthen economic growth for all".[1]

Despite the overall decrease in collective bargaining coverage, there have been some gains. Some public service unions in Europe have negotiated for an end to wage freezes, the introduction of new measures to compensate for pay cuts, and in some countries, there have been extensions of collective bargaining in the public sector. According to EPSU, governments in Germany, France and Estonia recently promoted collective bargaining in the public sector, and in the Netherlands, collective bargaining has been extended to new groups of workers to ensure social security coverage. In Ireland, workers gained the right to bargain collectively under new legislation introduced in 2015. The extension of collective bargaining rights in the public sector in Europe, Oceania and Latin America, in a large number of African countries and in some Asian countries (ILO 2013a), has benefited women workers as they represent a high percentage of public sector workers. Some of the agreements, resulting from the extension of bargaining coverage in the public sector, are discussed in Chapter 3.

In ten countries,[2] government policy measures and interventions by the social partners have recently extended collective bargaining coverage (Visser, Hayter & Gammarano 2015). In Switzerland and Norway, collective agreements have been extended to cover small businesses. In other countries, collective agreement coverage has increased as a result of economic growth and the increase in formal employment, for example, in Chile and as was previously the case, in Brazil. In a few countries, for example, France, Italy, Austria, Belgium and Canada, collective bargaining coverage remained relatively stable despite the economic crisis, owing to a continued willingness to regulate the labour market through collective bargaining (Visser, Hayter & Gammarano 2015).

---

1. See https://payrise.eu/news/trade-unions-issue-emergency-alert/ (accessed 24 September 2018).
2. Australia, the Netherlands, Brazil, Switzerland, Finland, Denmark, Malta, Chile, Iceland, France.

However, there are also significant setbacks, for example, in the USA when a Supreme Court ruling in June 2018 (*Janus v. AFSCME Council 31*) held that requiring fair share fees in the public sector violates the First Amendment of the Constitution. This ruling effectively nationalized right-to-work conditions across the public sector. All public sector non-union workers now have the right to opt out of paying a union fee if they benefit from a collective agreement. Previously this situation existed in six states only. The ruling could result in a decrease in public sector membership as well as a significant drop in union income. It strikes down the 40-year long recognition of the right to charge a fee to workers covered by collective agreements in the public sector although they are not union members.

2. SUPPORTIVE LEGISLATION ON GENDER EQUALITY

Supportive legal and policy frameworks for both gender equality and collective bargaining can give critical stimulus to the social partners to negotiate on key equality issues (Eurofound 2014a). The law can also open spaces for women to influence bargaining agendas in their unions. Dickens (1998) argues that, "in many cases a legal framework favourable to equality measures appears to have been necessary, if far from sufficient, to get the social partners to address equality issues in bargaining" (1998: 20).

In recent years proactive legislation has been introduced in many countries. Adherence to the ILO's Decent Work Agenda and ratification of core ILO Conventions on fundamental rights at work has also been important. Securing the legal rights to freedom of association and collective bargaining – enshrined in ILO Conventions Nos. 87, 98, 151 and 154 – has been fundamental for the capacity of unions to involve women in negotiations and include gender issues on the bargaining agenda.

In Europe, the law has played an important role in providing incentives and legitimizing collective bargaining (Deakin *et al.* 2015) and in some countries has formed the basis for union efforts in litigating on behalf of their members (Rubery 2016). One-quarter of unions responding to the

15

ETUC's "Bargaining for Equality" survey cited provisions in legislation for collective agreements on gender equality, for example, for company equality plans, measures to reduce pay inequalities, wage transparency, and reconciliation of work and family life, as being critical for collective bargaining (Pillinger 2014).

Legislation that supports the social partners, encourages them to bargain for equality, and places legal obligations on them to implement equality, can play an important role in institutionalizing bargaining for equality (Bleijenbergh, de Bruijn & Dickens 2001; Eurofound 2014a; Pillinger 2014). In some countries, for example, France, Spain and Italy, collective bargaining has been an important tool to implement equality legislation, particularly where it requires the social partners to agree equality measures. Union negotiating positions have been strengthened when bargaining on gender equality is specified, leading to collective agreements frequently extending rights beyond those set out in legislation (Deakin *et al.* 2015).

In Europe, strong legal frameworks established by some governments, EU directives on gender equality and the EU's commitment to social dialogue have helped to strengthen gender equality provisions in CBAs. Examples include requirements for employers to cooperate with unions in drawing up equality plans in France, Finland, Sweden, Austria and Spain. In countries with low collective bargaining coverage, trade unions have used the law to promote equality (for example, through litigation under equal pay legislation in the UK, USA and in Ontario and Quebec in Canada). In the UK, litigation and collective bargaining are viewed as complementary, with litigation considered a "potent mechanism for advancing social rights" (Deakin *et al.* 2015: 382). Briskin (2006) found that in Canada unions have given greater priority to government policy interventions and legal reforms, for example, in advocating for strengthened laws and public duties on implementing equal pay for work of equal value, because of the relatively limited scope of collective bargaining. In contrast in Sweden, stronger unions and centralized bargaining structures have resulted in unions prioritizing collective bargaining over legislation.

THE IMPORTANCE OF STRONG LEGAL FRAMEWORKS
ON GENDER EQUALITY

Trade unions in Canada were at the forefront in winning proactive legislation in Ontario, by requiring employers with more than ten employees to implement pay equity, under the Pay Equity Act, 1990 and the Employment Standards Act, 2000, with a model of pay equity that was adopted in other states. In Ontario, new rules were introduced in 2018 to extend equal pay to part-time and casual workers at the same rate as full-time workers for the same rate of pay. The amendment to the Act arose because part-time workers doing the same work as full-time workers were being paid minimum wages. In 2018, the Canadian Union of Public Employees (CUPE) challenged an amendment in 2009 to the Quebec Pay Equity Act by the Liberal Government. The court ruled that the amendment to the Act had been unconstitutional, denying women the right to be paid fairly according to the value of their work.

In Canada, sustained union campaigns led to an amendment to the Ontario Occupational Health and Safety Act in 2010, which mandates employers and unions to prevent sexual harassment and violence, and provides for paid leave of five days if a woman has experienced domestic violence in the workplace. Similar state legislation has been passed in Manitoba and Alberta. In Manitoba, for example, a worker can request up to 17 weeks unpaid leave without it jeopardizing their employment. Amendments to the Labour Code in 2018 provided workers in federally-regulated workplaces with the right to five days paid leave, and up to ten days of additional unpaid leave, if they have experienced domestic violence. In 2018, the right to ten days paid leave for victims of domestic violence was granted in legislation in New Zealand, under the Domestic Violence Victims' Protection Bill.

Legislation in Italy and Spain on the right to paid leave for victims of domestic violence has been an important driver for trade union negotiations to consolidate these rights in collective bargaining and in some cases to extend the minimum established in the law (Pillinger 2017a).

In Australia, the Equal Opportunities for Women in the Workplace Act 1999 requires employers to draw up equal opportunities policies. As a result, significant new rights for all workers with childcare responsibilities have been delivered through litigation, such as the work and family test case in 2005 that resulted in the increase in unpaid parental leave, the right to request flexible working time and carer's leave entitlements (Parker *et al.* 2011).

In 2017, UNISON in the UK won a significant legal case in the Supreme Court, reversing a change in the law on the implementation of fees for cases taken before industrial tribunals. This was particularly important, as unions in the UK have used litigation extensively to win rights for women workers. The Supreme Court unanimously ruled that the government was acting unlawfully and unconstitutionally and the government was also required to refund more than £27 million to people who had been charged fees since the law changed in July 2013. The introduction of fees had particularly affected cases taken by low-paid women who had faced discrimination and unequal pay.

While bargaining can play a decisive role in the implementation of legislation and extending legal provisions to secure substantive rights for women workers, in some cases trade unions and employers may only engage in bargaining when the law requires this on a particular topic. There can be reluctance within some trade unions to move beyond existing legal requirements on gender equality. In part, this is indicative of a resistance to extending bargaining into new arenas, but also because of the generalized push-back and decentralization of bargaining in some countries since the economic crisis.

3. EXTENDING THE SCOPE AND REACH OF COLLECTIVE BARGAINING

Globalization and neoliberalism pose major challenges to bargaining because of the significant changes in the structure and organization of work, with a shift of production from developed to developing countries, organized through complex global supply chains and in export processing zones (EPZs) in sectors such as agriculture, electronics and garments (Asia Wage Floor Alliance *et al.* 2018; Davies 2000; Evers, Amoding & Krishnan 2014; OECD *et al.* 2014; Oxfam International 2004; Staritz & Guilherme Reis 2013).

In recent years, union organizing strategies have included groups of women workers who in the past were outside the traditional scope and coverage of collective bargaining. Faced with new organizing and bargaining challenges, union campaigns have focused on low-paid care workers, part-time workers and workers on casual contracts, and the extension of the scope of collective bargaining, for example, concerning the rights of part-time workers. In some developing countries, recent union and NGO mobilizing has led to innovative strategies ranging from organizing and bargaining for informal workers in markets or street vendors to representing low-paid women garment workers in export-orientated factories.

Unions have also extended the scope and reach of bargaining to workers in new forms of casual and flexible employment, known as the "gig" economy (Moore 2018). Unions have developed new strategies to provide workers with rights (OECD 2018). Examples include some breakthroughs led by unions in the UK, over the taxi app Uber and the food delivery company Deliveroo, amongst others in securing employment rights for workers. The Austrian union Vida has established a works' council for Foodora (food delivery) riders and plans to negotiate a collective agreement for bicycle delivery services (Vida 2017).

However, many women across the world are either excluded from collective bargaining coverage because of limitations on the right to freedom of association and collective bargaining and/or because they work in jobs or sectors that traditionally are outside of the reach and coverage of collective bargaining. For this reason, women working in precarious jobs, women working in informal work, and women from racialized and migrant backgrounds, are frequently not covered by collective bargaining nor receive support and solidarity from trade unions. This raises important questions about how to organize workers with limited bargaining power (Blackett & Sheppard 2003).

In some countries, women have been more successful in their representation in tripartite bodies, compared to bipartite collective bargaining, as is the case in Uruguay through the Tripartite Commission for Equal Opportunities at Work (Espina & Pedetti 2012). Unions in MNEs have negotiated global framework agreements and some regional and joint declarations. Some focus on female-dominated sectors, such as garments, electronics and agricultural sectors.

4. QUALITY PUBLIC SERVICES AND PROGRESSIVE SOCIAL POLICY AND FISCAL FRAMEWORKS

Universal quality public services benefit women and are of major importance to the achievement of gender equality. Gender-responsive public services are closely connected to progressive national social policies that promote equality in areas such as equal sharing of paid parental leave, subsidized childcare, provision of elderly care, rights to flexible work, measures to compensate for unpaid care work through payments or social protection, and to ensuring women's safety and freedom from gender-based violence in public places (Elson & Pearson 2015; PSI 2017; Rubery 2016; Williams 2016). Access to gender-responsive public services (GRPS) to support women's equal participation in employment has been a strong focus of union campaigns, and particularly the Public Services International (PSI) global campaign for quality public services. PSI has campaigned for universal access to health and social protection, and rights-based and gender-responsive approaches to migration. As the PSI's Programme of Action 2018–22 argues:

> There can be no gender equality without economic justice, universal access to quality public services and women's control of their bodies ... Public provision of affordable, high-quality childcare, improved parental paid leave and other family supports remove barriers to women's participation in the workforce, improve economic equality and create stronger economies and more resilient societies (PSI 2017: para. 3.2).

Gender responsive quality public services reduce inequalities in access to education and health services, and provide decent work opportunities for women (EI 2017; PSI 2018). Investment in public services reduces inequality and promotes women's entry into the labour market (Martinez-Vazquez 2012; Oxfam 2018; PSI 2017). Measures such as free or subsidized childcare provision and paid parental leave promote women and men's equal participation in the labour market and reduce the motherhood pay gap (Fagan, Hegewisch & Pillinger 2006). Quality public services also provide safety and security from gender-based violence and women's access to justice (ITUC 2017; UN Women 2017). In Cambodia, for example, investments in public services and support services benefit women garment workers, who are at a constant risk of violence – including rape and sexual assault – when they travel to and from work (Action Aid 2017).

Furthermore, without substantial reforms and a social investment strategy, the achievement of the UN's Sustainable Development Goals will be aspirational (Donald & Moussie 2016). This is particularly relevant to Goal 5 to "achieve gender equality and empower all women and girls", where governments are committed to "recognize and value unpaid care and domestic work through the provision of public services, infrastructure and social protection policies and the promotion of shared responsibility within the household and the family as nationally appropriate". Because tax policies play a crucial role in determining inequalities of all kinds, including the financial incentives for women to enter paid employment, progressive national tax reforms and individualized tax systems are vital to effect positive change (European Commission 2017c).

Global unions are strong advocates within the emerging global movement for universal social protection floors and for tax policies that generate sufficient funding for quality public services (PSI 2017). The Global Alliance for Tax Justice, founded in Lima, Peru in 2013, with 81 organizations across the world from civil society and trade unions in five regional networks, advocates for a fair, transparent and equitable tax system to fund vital public services for all, redistribution of tax benefits, more progressive tax policies and an end to tax havens.

5. ADDRESSING WOMEN'S UNPAID CARE WORK AND STRUCTURAL INEQUALITIES

Women's unpaid care work

Women's unpaid care work impacts on "the ability, duration and types of work opportunities which women are able to take advantage of, reinforcing gender gaps in occupations, pay and career development" (ILO 2018c: 1). In the EU, it is estimated that the value of unpaid family care and domestic work taken together ranges between 27.1 per cent and 37 per cent of EU gross domestic product (GDP) (European Parliament 2009). In Peru, it is estimated that women's unpaid care work could represent as much as 20 per cent of GDP (Antonopoulos & Hirway 2009). Women's unpaid care work results in time poverty and resource poverty, trapping women in unequal gender roles, and precarious and informal work (Action Aid 2013; Blackden & Wodon 2006; Fraser 2011; UN Women 2015). The UN Special Rapporteur on extreme poverty and human rights (UN General Assembly 2013) has defined care as a human rights issue, positioning unpaid care work as a major barrier to decent work, and ultimately the realization of women's economic, political and cultural rights.

Some unions have raised awareness of the inherent inequalities that arise from women's unpaid care work. PSI, for example, has argued for the introduction of "gender sensitive policies that take account of the constraints and the discrimination faced by women and of the unpaid care work carried out by women" (PSI 2014: 1). In the absence of quality public services, women bear a far greater burden of unpaid care, and cuts in and privatization of services have the effect of forcing women back into unpaid care roles, further reinforcing gender inequalities (Jaysinghe 2014). Women with care roles are vulnerable to exploitation in the informal labour market, particularly when they combine unpaid and paid work such as homework and night shifts. Parental leave, childcare, social protection and the redistribution of time are key issues for bargaining because they give recognition to the unequal distribution of unpaid care work and the importance of social policies that support care provision. As the ILO (2018c: 2) argues, transformative policies are needed in the context of the future of work. Furthermore, when "care policies redistribute care provision between women and men and between households and the society at large" they ensure the "wellbeing of societies".

Research commissioned by the International Trade Union Confederation (ITUC) indicates that increasing investment in public services would stimulate employment and economic growth and the provision of collectivized care services, child and elder care in the care industry (De Henau, Perrons & Himmelweit 2017). ITUC has highlighted the importance of women's care work in "The Decent Work, Decent Life for Women" campaign, which includes promoting the ratification of ILO Convention 183 on Maternity Protection, as well as pay equity and balancing family and work commitments. In addition, there are often the fiscal disincentives to secondary earners built into the majority of family-based personal tax systems (European Commission 2017c).

Gender mainstreaming strategies in trade unions: a tool to address structural inequalities?

Gender mainstreaming is a tool for integrating gender into all policies and practices and has a transformative and long-term approach towards achieving gender equality. Unlike the equal treatment approach (equality of opportunity), it goes further in examining the underlying reasons for gender inequality (Rees 1998). In a union context, the focus has been on how to integrate gender into internal decision-making structures, union policies and in the formulation of collective bargaining claims, negotiations and in the evaluation of their outcomes. Unions have also played a role in lobbying and campaigning for gender mainstreaming in national law and policy, recognizing at the same time that trade unions are important partners in this work, particularly where it concerns macroeconomic policy, budgeting and the implementation of policies affecting gender equality in employment and the workplace.

Many governments have now adopted some form of "gender budgeting", in relation to specific taxes, or social security measures, or spending on public services. But this is rarely extended to the macroeconomics of the budget, to the decisions on how the size of the budget deficit, if at all, should be reduced, and by what mix of spending cuts and tax increases. Analysis by the independent UK Women's Budget Group has shown the consequences for gender equality of drastic austerity measures and changes to delivery of social security in the UK (Women's Budget Group 2016, 2017).

The first international commitment on gender mainstreaming under the UN's Fourth World Conference on Women (Beijing 1995) Platform for Action acknowledged the role of trade unions, calling on governments and all social actors to recognise collective bargaining as a right and an important mechanism for the promotion of gender equality. In Europe, the European Commission (1996) communication on gender mainstreaming embedded gender mainstreaming as a policy priority, for example, as seen most recently as a goal in the European Commission's (2016) Strategic Engagement for Gender Equality 2016–18. Grünell's (2006) analysis of the social partners found that gender mainstreaming in collective bargaining was on the agenda of union confederations of the 17 EU countries and Norway studied, whereas employers preferred individual solutions rather than general rules.

However, gender mainstreaming has been poorly implemented owing to a combination of a lack of commitment, expertise or resources, and resistance within organizations. It has often been treated as a technical exercise, rather than a transformative tool for achieving gender equality. Despite more than two decades of union policy commitments, training and guidance on gender mainstreaming in collective bargaining, there is still a failure to systematically integrate a gender analysis into collective bargaining (Pillinger 2014). Although some pay negotiations have included a gender mainstreaming approach, with objectives to reduce the gender pay gap, in the public sector in particular, this has barely impacted on entrenched structural inequalities such as occupational segregation, women's care responsibilities, low pay and undervaluation of women's work and the growth of insecure and precarious work (Pillinger 2018).

Persistent occupational segregation and under-representation of women in decision-making remain significant barriers to mainstreaming gender equality into negotiations (Briskin & Muller 2011; Budlender 2010, Grünell 2006; Parker *et al.* 2011), resulting in weak linkages between government programmes and collective bargaining (Grünell & Schaapman 2005).

At the European level, the limited progress in gender mainstreaming is a reflection of political contradictions between the pursuit of the European social model and the promotion of neoliberal economic policies (Wickham 2005). Overall, the implementation of gender mainstreaming in the context of European policy making has been slow and disappointing (Plantenga, Remery & Rubery 2006) and in relation to European employment policy is considered "incomplete" (Fagan & Rubery 2017). Fagan and Rubery's (2017) analysis of the effects of Brexit and "decoupling from the EU's equality framework" may well further harm the pursuit of gender equality in the UK.

Some successes can be found in the operational programmes of EU structural funds and their implementation in member states, promoted through the EU-wide community of practice (CoP) on gender mainstreaming, an EU learning network for managing authorities, and through training under the European structural fund (ESF) "Gender mainstreaming into practice" project. There are some good examples from municipalities in Sweden and Finland of how gender mainstreaming has been included in the design, planning and running of municipal services, with involvement of trade unions. Unions in Europe also see the recent policy developments and in particular the 2017 European pillar of social rights, which aims to create more inclusive labour markets and reduce precarious work, as an opportunity for a reinvigorated gender-mainstreaming approach (EPSU 2018).

Examples of union policy commitments include training and guidelines for collective bargaining teams, carried out by nearly half of unions in the ETUC's "Bargaining for Equality" survey (Pillinger 2014). More unions now carry out gender-impact assessments of collective agreements, on the grounds that the formulation and preparation of collective bargaining claims is neither gender-neutral nor automatically inclusive of the voice and agency of all women.

Some unions have carried out gender-impact assessment of collective agreements prior to their renegotiation or when agreements are updated, as is the case, for example, in Spain, Germany, Finland, Sweden, Denmark and Norway. Others have carried out studies to assess the content of existing collective agreements, as is the case in Italy (Leonardi & de Srio 2012). The aim is to ensure that women's needs and concerns are included and that discriminatory clauses and unintended gender bias is removed. Further examples are found in the box below.

EXAMPLES OF GENDER MAINSTREAMING IN UNION POLICIES

Public Services International (PSI): In 2002, PSI was the first Global Union Federation (GUF) to adopt a policy on gender mainstreaming designed to encourage its affiliates to introduce a gender perspective in all policies, programmes and in collective bargaining (PSI 2002). At the same time, PSI amended its constitution to guarantee 50 per cent participation of women in all its decision-making bodies (Wintour 2011).

European Federation of Public Service Unions (EPSU): EPSU's gender main-streaming audit (EPSU 2010) gives evidence of how gender equality is integrated into a trade union's policy framework and core activities, such as its constitution, congress resolutions, policies and programmes, and social dialogue committee activities. In 2017, the EPSU congress adopted a reso-lution and roadmap on gender equality and women's rights, calling for "revi-talizing the commitment to gender equality in times of crisis" (EPSU 2017). In February 2018, an EPSU European gender equality conference adopted a two-pronged commitment to gender mainstreaming through internal measures (trade union decision-making and policies) and external measures (EU and member states).

European Trade Union Confederation (ETUC): In 2007, the ETUC adopted a "Charter on Gender-Mainstreaming in Trade Unions" with a specific sec-tion on gender mainstreaming in collective bargaining. Gender parity in decision-making structures was achieved in the ETUC in 2018. The ETUC Paris action programme (2015–19) and the ETUC action programme on gender equality (2016–19), includes six priorities: mainstreaming gender into all ETUC policies; achieving equal pay between women and men; eliminating the gender gap in decision-making bodies; tackling the challenge of work–life balance; facilitating work, family and private life; and addressing the link between domestic violence and workplace rights. The ETUC launched a pay rise campaign in 2016 to respond to the unacceptable drop in wages over the last decade in Europe and to address inequalities in wage share, the gen-der pay gap, and massive wage divergences across Europe.

Icelandic Confederation of Labour: guidelines to promote gender main-streaming in bargaining teams were drawn up as part of the collective agree-ments negotiated in 2008 and 2010. The confederation's equality and family committee provided special training courses on gender mainstreaming in collective bargaining and in women's empowerment.

Finland – Collective Agreement for Government Employees for 2010–12: the Finnish Government Employees Union was the first union to carry out a gender impact assessment with a particular focus on the gender impact of pay and working time agreements. Gender impact assessments have also been carried out under the 2010–11 collective agreement for health services employees, collective agreements in the hotel and catering sector, and the collective agreement of the Employers' Association for Service Enterprises.

Belgian confederations (ACV/CSC, ABVV/FGTB and ACLVB/CGSLB): gender mainstreaming was introduced in 2004 through a joint charter and declaration on gender mainstreaming by the three Belgium national confederations to assist unions in integrating gender into collective bargaining, starting with the representation of women in their own organizations. Collective agreements were assessed for their gender impact; collective bargaining teams were trained in gender-mainstreaming techniques and a handbook produced to guide negotiators.

A further Belgian confederation, the CNE, published a report setting out proposals for negotiations in its paper "Equality, unfinished mission: proposals for the 2013–2014 negotiations in sectors and companies" providing objectives and guidance on how to negotiate on equality. It includes practical guidelines for union negotiators in the areas of women's part-time work, occupational segregation, reconciliation of work and family life, the undervaluing of women's work, and gender disaggregated data and wage transparency.

Training for works' council members, negotiating guidelines and tools to identify gender-discriminatory clauses in collective agreements have been drawn up by the ÖGB, the Austrian trade union confederation. The Spanish metalworking union MCA-UGT prepares annual guidelines and training for negotiators on gender issues for collective bargaining. In the UK, the TUC carries out an equality audit every two years to monitor progress on equality and equality bargaining across multiple grounds of discrimination (women workers, migrant workers, black and minority ethnic workers, disabled workers, older and younger workers and LGBT workers) (TUC 2016).

---

6. GENDER RESPONSIVE TRADE UNIONS: POLICIES, TOOLS, TRAINING AND INTERNAL STRUCTURES

Gender equality in union strategic priorities and policies

A study by Eurofound (2014) of EU countries found that in 17 EU countries the social partners had well-developed policies on gender equality; in seven countries initiatives were limited to measures taken by unions;

and in a further four countries there were no policy or priority measure on gender equality. In general, social partners had better-developed
external policies on gender equality compared to internal equality performance measures, such as the representation of women in
decision-making positions. Overall, internal policies tended to be better
developed in union organizations compared to employers' organizations.
Women's campaigning and organizing has resulted in unions addressing
gender biases and gendered roles and norms, and improved women's
representation in collective bargaining. Despite positive developments,
many challenges remain; not least in addressing a lack of political will in
some unions, persistence of gender stereotypes and a lack of priority and
resources devoted to gender equality.

Guidelines and training programmes on gender equality

Guidelines and training on gender equality and equal pay, including
gender mainstreaming tools, for collective bargaining teams have been
put in place by over half of national confederations in Europe (Pillinger
2014) and are increasingly common elsewhere. Nearly half of European
trade unions responding to the ETUC's "Bargaining for Equality" survey had introduced gender equality and gender-mainstreaming training
for bargaining teams, 40 per cent had introduced specific guidelines for
bargaining teams on how to integrate a gender perspective into collective bargaining and 38 per cent reported on measures to improve the
representation of women in collective bargaining teams. A number of
other actions were reported by unions, including specific activities to
monitor the potential discriminatory content of collective agreements,
campaigns on equal pay and pay inequalities, studies and data collection,
the development of certification systems, the publication of model gender equality clauses for collective agreements and influencing national
legislation and policy.

Outside Europe, trade unions have also been active in carrying out
training programmes, developing guidelines and training manuals and
implementing women's leadership courses, sometimes with a specific

focus on developing equality bargaining proposals. In relation to bargaining topics, it has been easier to gain gender equality "wins" by focusing on the "softer" areas of gender equality such as work–life balance, where often common ground can be found within the union itself and with employers (Eurofound 2014a).

EXAMPLES OF TOOLS AND TRAINING TO MAKE COLLECTIVE BARGAINING GENDER-RESPONSIVE

The global union, Union Network International (UNI) has developed a "gender-take away package" with information and training on how unions can include gender mainstreaming into their work and in collective bargaining.

The ITUC's "Decisions for Life" campaign focused on organizing young women in the service sectors in 14 countries in order to improve their working conditions and to increase young women's union membership (ITUC 2011b). An ITUC campaign guide was produced in 2013 with a focus on young women's empowerment and encouragement to take up leadership positions and engage in union reform.

The South African Commercial, Catering and Allied Workers Union's (SACCAWU) has carried out campaigns and training programmes, and has drawn up a model bargaining claim, on parental rights.

In several countries, women's leadership development programmes have been important to encouraging women to take up decision-making positions. In the case of the Australian Education Union (AEU) programme, online support networks encourage women into leadership positions.

In Colombia in 2014, the national trade union centres (CUT and CTC) with the support of global unions organized a national meeting of women leaders entitled "Women who transform trade unionism" to draw up a roadmap for integrating equality into collective bargaining. A wide range of strategies were agreed from awareness-raising campaigns and training on gender equality; valuing women's work; development of company equality plans; ensuring collective bargaining is gender sensitive; and strengthening women's departments in the unions.

In Brazil, the national women's department of the CUT (SNMT-CUT) carried out training programmes and guidance for women leaders at national and regional levels. At the 2012 congress the CUT voted to achieve gender parity in its leadership structures. A list of model gender equality clauses has been drawn up on access to training and promotion, revision of salary scales in female-dominated sectors, maternity and paternity benefits, occupational safety and health, and sexual harassment.

Model clauses

Model clauses have been used by many unions as a way of improving familiarity with the language of gender equality. In Australia, a model clause on domestic violence at work was one of the enablers for a substantial number of enterprise agreements on domestic violence leave (discussed further in Chapter 3). The TUC in the UK has drawn up a model equality clause for internal trade union policies specifying that the objects of the union will include: the promotion of equality for all including through collective bargaining and the union's own employment practices; and to oppose actively all forms of harassment. It aims to ensure that equality is mainstreamed through all union activities, including collective bargaining. By 2014 three-quarters of unions affiliated to the TUC had adopted the clause (TUC 2014).

7. WOMEN'S REPRESENTATION IN UNION DECISION-MAKING AND IN COLLECTIVE BARGAINING TEAMS

When women are in leadership positions, social partner organizations are more likely to have developed gender equality strategies and policies (ETUC 2010, 2017b; Eurofound 2014a). However, unequal power relations in the workplace and in union structures, particularly in male-dominated industries such as printing have been significant barriers to equality (Dawson 2018).

In many regions trade unions are developing policies and structures that aim to promote women's participation in decision-making, for example, through women's leadership training programmes, women's or gender equality structures and through quota systems for women's representation and participation. Changes to trade union rule books, including quotas, reserved seats or proportional representation, have the effect of increasing union democracy and ensuring that women can enter senior union positions (ETUC 2010; Ledwith 2006).

For example, the principle of proportionality in decision-making bodies was first adopted by two UK trade unions (GPMU and UNISON) in the 1990s. In Latin America, quotas were also introduced: a 20 per cent women's quota was introduced by the CTA in Argentina in 1992 and a 30 per cent quota was introduced in Brazil in 1993. At the 2012 congress, the CUT in Chile, which already had 30 per cent women's participation in its decision-making structures, voted for a resolution to achieve gender parity by the next congress. Globally, nearly 40 per cent of education unions have introduced a gender quota system for women's representation in the highest decision-making body (Wintour 2015). Women's quotas have had a positive effect both on women's representation and on organizational outcomes, indicating that changes in union governance can contribute to union revitalization (Kirsch & Blaschke 2014).

The ETUC's equality surveys find that many unions are introducing strategies and policies to improve gender balance, with three-quarters of confederations having a specific policy designed to increase the presence of women in their decision-making bodies (ETUC, 2008–17). The 2017 ETUC Equality Survey (ETUC 2017b) confirmed that the average percentage of women in the membership of unions was 45.1 per cent (based on 38 confederations providing information). However, women held only 23.9 per cent of union leadership positions.

In the ETUC and in some European federations, women now make up a growing share of leadership positions. In Australia, for example, the number of senior women union leaders is notable and the union bargaining agendas are clearly mainstreaming gender and other diversity issues, and taking the lead on introducing new issues onto the agenda, particularly in relation to domestic violence. A survey carried out for Education International (Wintour 2015) found that gender parity in union decision-making structures in many OECD countries has largely been achieved and women's or gender advisory structures have transitioned from working on issues around women's participation in unions and leadership to focus more on professional issues, such as gender relations in schools and in classrooms. The EI survey also found that by 2010, 44.6 per cent of affiliated education unions had achieved gender parity on their executive boards, with 50 per cent or more female representation. This figure increased to 50.9 per cent by 2014. However, if the goal is to reach representation proportionate to female membership, there is still some distance to travel.

However, there are still many cases of male-dominated unions, which fail to give voice and representation to women. Evans (2017) found that women's priorities were often ignored and union leaders, for example, in Bangladesh and Cambodia failed to listen to women. She argues that: "If women perceive unions as unresponsive, they may be reluctant to approach representatives and engage in union activities" (10).

Women's representation in collective-bargaining

Women's presence in collective bargaining makes a significant difference in the promotion of equality, in agenda-setting and in achieving outcomes in equality bargaining (Colgan & Ledwith 1996; Dickens 2000; ETUC 2010; Ledwith & Munakamwe 2015; Pillinger 2014). Gender balance in collective bargaining teams enables new perspectives to be integrated into the collective bargaining agenda, which can enrich and promote new approaches to collective bargaining, and change culture and attitudes, by drawing on women's experiences and knowledge.

Women not only highlight new issues and agendas for bargaining, when they participate in negotiations, collective agreements are more likely to address gender equality considerations (Dickens 1998; ETUC 2010; Pillinger, Schmidt & Wintour 2016). An important precondition for the preparation of collective bargaining claims is to ensure that women's voices are heard and that there is active participation of women in union decision-making structures both in formulating claims and in negotiating teams (Briskin 2006; ILO 2002, 2014). In the ETUC "Bargaining for Equality" survey (Pillinger 2014) a large number of unions highlighted the importance of women's presence in collective bargaining teams as being a prerequisite for bargaining to reduce pay inequalities between women and men. However, just fewer than 40 per cent of unions responding to the survey had put in place policies or strategies to improve the representation of women in collective bargaining teams.

CONCLUSION

This chapter has discussed the preconditions for gender equality to be integrated into collective bargaining and has argued that there is strong potential for collective bargaining to promote gender equality at work. Collective bargaining should be viewed as part of a wider range of institutional mechanisms, including proactive gender equality legislation, economic, employment and social policies, along with gender-responsive public services, to address structural gender inequalities in the labour market. This integrated and interrelated approach to rights, employment protection and social dialogue is reflected in the ILO's 2008 Declaration on Social Justice for a Fair Globalization.

Although collective bargaining is generally underutilized as a tool for achieving equality (Dickens 2000), it has enormous potential to promote equality at all bargaining levels, particularly because bargaining offers certain advantages over legislation and gives voice to women that reflects the realities of their working lives. However, as Cynthia Cockburn (1991) argues, there is a need to move beyond women being accommodated in male-dominated organizational structures and cultures.

Despite the economic crisis and declining trade union density, there have been some recent transformations in bargaining reflecting women's voice, gender mainstreaming and intersectional approaches, and making connections between women's unpaid care work and paid employment.

3

Collective bargaining as a tool for gender equality: evidence from across the world

Collective bargaining can ensure the systematic integration of gender dimensions into labour market and macroeconomic policies in general, and address specific issues such as the gender pay gap, enhanced protection against discrimination, work–family measures and childcare infrastructure, sexual violence and harassment, and the promotion of female employment. (ILO 2009 Resolution concerning "Gender equality at the heart of decent work", para. 37).

This chapter discusses three main themes that are important components of recent bargaining and collective agreements on gender equality: (1) closing the gender pay gap; (2) maternity protection, parental leave and work–life balance; and (3) gender-based violence at work. Despite the external environment leading to the decentralization and weakening of bargaining in many countries across the world, in recent years bargaining has become more gender-focused. The bargaining agenda has been extended to include new issues that reflect the intersection of the private area of family/home and the public area of work, thereby extending the scope of the employment relationship. In particular, domestic violence is a new workplace bargaining issue that "widens the reach of the employment relationship by recognizing the intersection of the private and work domains and represents a qualitative new step" (Pillinger, Schmidt & Wintour 2016).

CLOSING THE GENDER PAY GAP THROUGH
COLLECTIVE BARGAINING

Collective bargaining has played a role in closing the gender pay gap, and as discussed previously, there is wide agreement that centralized bargaining generally has a positive impact on gender pay inequalities (Hayter 2011; Pillinger 2014; Ponzellini, Aumayr & Wolf 2010). A reduction in the gender pay gap from 2004 to 2008 can be attributed to three main factors: (1) working in the public sector; (2) membership of a trade union; and (3) working in a large firm (Olsen *et al.* 2010). The success of bargaining strategies is dependent on a range of factors (discussed in Chapter 1), as well as the level of union commitment to the issue and the proportion of women in a sector (Dawson 2018; Elvira & Saporta 2001; Rubery & Koukiadaki 2016).

However, the trend towards the individualization of pay and a lack of pay transparency makes the issue of pay inequalities between women and men complex to tackle, particularly in the context of the economic crisis and a general trend towards rising wage inequalities (Antonczyk *et al.* 2010). Widening wage inequalities between and within firms has also been associated with the decline in collective regulation and of sector-wide bargaining in the private sector, which has most affected those at the bottom of the wage structure (Rubery & Grimshaw 2014).

There is also evidence of substantial gender bias in the distribution of bonuses and performance-related pay (Pillinger 2014; Rubery & Grimshaw 2014; Wintour 2015). The recent publication of the wide gender pay gaps in UK companies with over 250 employees, such as banking and media, as a result of the introduction of new mandatory reporting requirements, confirms the significance of bonuses and performance-related pay in explaining the gender pay gap.

Trade union strategies on equal pay first focused on equal wage rates for men and women performing the same job (Tzannatos & Zabalza 1985). This issue has largely been superseded although wage differentials based on gender alone still exist in some precarious work settings, such as building sites in south east Asia. In many developing countries, it is not uncommon to find direct discrimination in the allocation of certain benefits, including in the public sector. For example, in many developing countries, while basic pay may be equal, the extensive use of benefits, such as family benefits regarding housing, funeral grants and health insurance, can directly discriminate against women. For example, education unions in some African countries are addressing issues of direct pay discrimination against women with regards to certain benefits, for example, child allowances are only paid to male employees; and medical expenses are paid to a male employee for his wife and children but not to a female employee if her spouse is not working (Wintour 2015).

However, in general, the focus has moved to challenges relating to occupational segregation, equal pay for work of equal value, and gender bias in job classification schemes. In OECD countries, from the 1970s until the 2008 economic crisis, the gender pay gap became an increasing priority issue for trade unions, particularly in the Nordic countries, western Europe, Canada and the USA, often in alliance with national equality bodies or the women's movement. However, since 2008, employers' demands for cost neutral adjustments have often meant that the pay gap is given less priority in bargaining for fear of wage levelling down (Karamessini & Rubery 2014; Perrons & Plomient 2014).

A consistent finding from the ETUC's "Bargaining for Equality" survey of trade unions across Europe is that collective bargaining, particularly centralized and sectoral bargaining, impacted on women's pay across the economy, and represents "the most effective way that unions can implement actions to reduce pay inequalities between women and men" (Pillinger 2014: 27). Table 3.1 below shows the main results from the ETUC's survey of the types of agreements that had been negotiated in order to reduce pay inequalities between women and men.

Legal and other incentives have proved an important mechanism to focus employers and unions on bargaining to close the gender pay gap, as exists in some European countries (Belgium, France, Finland, Germany and Sweden) where specific incentives exist to carry out equal pay bargaining, as part of tripartite social dialogue. For example, in Belgium and France, there are obligatory negotiating duties for the social partners on the issue of equal pay. In particular, collective bargaining had the biggest impact where gender-specific pay bargaining

Table 3.1: Collective agreements to reduce pay inequalities between women and men

	Confederations*	Federations	All
Reconciliation of work/family life	51% (18)	42% (5)	49% (23)
Training and career development	43% (15)	25% (3)	38% (18)
Pay increase low-paid workers	34% (12)	17% (2)	30% (14)
Low pay of women in female-dominated sectors	20% (9)	0%	20% (9)
Transparency in pay systems/job classification	26% (9)	25% (3)	26% (12)
Pay surveys/pay audit	23% (8)	25% (3)	23% (11)
Job evaluation/low value of women's work	20% (7)	25% (3)	21% (10)
Gender sensitivity in performance-related pay	6% (2)	0%	4% (2)
Other	6% (2)	25% (3)	11% (5)

Source: Pillinger 2014.

* A confederation usually refers to a cross-sectoral national trade union body and a federation is usually a national sectoral or industry-based trade union, i.e. the Trades Union Congress (TUC) is a confederation and the National Union of Mineworkers (NUM) is a federation. However, in some countries, the national trade union centre may be called a federation. In this text, the standard definition applies.

objectives were introduced, with between one or two percentage points reduction in the gender pay gap in any given year (Pillinger 2014). In Norway, for example, collective bargaining is largely responsible for the progressive narrowing of the gender wage gap since 2008, and a bargaining objective for pay increases for women in female-dominated sectors resulted in one per cent reduction in the pay gap between 2010 and 2011, which also substantially reduced the numbers of low-paid women workers. In Finland, a one per cent reduction in the pay gap was also attributed to collective bargaining under the country's National Equal Pay programme. In the Czech Republic, in 2012, the Czech-Moravian Confederation of Trade Unions' (CMKOS) analysis of collective agreements found that increases in average wages and salaries at the median level in companies with a collective agreement were significantly more favourable than wages in companies where the collective agreement had not been concluded (Pillinger 2014). There is now some discussion also among political parties and trade unions about drafting a new law on wage transparency (European Commission 2016).

Unions representing workers in countries with a high gender pay gap have put more emphasis on the structural causes of pay inequalities, such as the undervaluing of women's work, occupational segregation and women's low pay. For example, in Germany, sectoral models of wage bargaining for industry-specific gender wage gaps have focused on living wages for skilled full-time employees (Schäfer & Gottschall 2015). In contrast, unions representing workers in countries with a lower gender pay gap (mainly countries in eastern and central Europe) have different negotiating strategies, often primarily focused on low pay, increasing minimum wages across the whole economy, and implementing policies on reconciliation of work and family life. Unions that have not negotiated agreements to reduce pay inequalities state that it is because of poor collective bargaining coverage generally and low employer engagement, rather than a lack of commitment to the goal of gender equality (Pillinger 2014).

In the public sector in Europe, closing the gender pay gap remains one of the most important equality issues in collective bargaining (EPSU 2013). An example in the UK is the Joint Higher Education Trade Union Pay Equality Claim 2015/16 by the trade unions, UCU, UNISON, Unite, EIS, GMB, where equal pay was a major part of the equality agenda, and which included commitments to address the undervaluing of women's work and company-level pay audits (ILO 2018). Some unions have been highly successful in concluding agreements and building capacity in sourcing and analyzing gender disaggregated data. For example, the regional collective agreement for Catalonia 2015–17 included an explicit objective to reduce the gender pay gap. In Denmark and Sweden, public sector unions representing low-paid female-dominated sectors, such as health and social care, are increasingly questioning the structural inequalities inherent in the Nordic collective bargaining model based on "pace setting", a formula for pay setting led by export-orientated industries in the private sector (Pillinger 2014). In November 2014 agreement was made with industrial employers to discuss the structure of wages in the economy and how they contribute to the gender pay gap. While the employers argued that the economy needs a strong and competitive export sector, Kommunal, the municipal workers' union, argued that industry's competitiveness depends on an effective social infrastructure that provides education and care for the young and the elderly (EPSU collective bargaining database).

Outside the OECD countries, there are some initiatives to address the gender wage gap but they are not widespread. The EI quadrennial equality survey (Wintour 2015) found that the great majority of unions addressing the gender pay gap were from Europe or other OECD countries. The report noted that there was still insufficient understanding of the terms gender pay and pay equity and many unions considered there was no gender pay gap in their country or sector. At a global level in the education sector, EI's quadrennial survey (Wintour 2015) found that 40 per cent of responding unions focused on issues related to the gender pay gap. Many unions seek to ensure that women are part of the unions' collective bargaining teams and are therefore able to monitor provisions on gender equality in collective agreements. However, only 23.7 per cent had included specific provisions in the collective bargaining claim designed to reduce the gender pay gap. Some unions were involved in lobbying parliaments or the European Parliament on equal pay issues or were part of broader union coalitions focusing on equal pay.

In Latin America, the majority of collective agreements include general non-discrimination clauses related to equal work for equal pay but not work of equal value, often reflecting existing deficiencies in labour codes or equality legislation. There have been some initiatives in the Southern Cone to address the pay gap. For example, in Argentina, the Labour Code article 172 requires the full observation of the principle of equal remuneration for work of equal value in the collective contracts and salary scales. In the textile sector, in 2012, a special bipartite commission was established in order to revise the job classifications and salary scales. The PIT-CNT in Uruguay negotiated a job evaluation system with the aim of eliminating salary differences between men and women. In Brazil, there have been some initiatives at state level. For example, the CUT in Quixadá, Brazil, as part of a public sector equality campaign, set up a commission on salary equality. New clauses on equal pay for work of equal value were then transposed into Law 2280/07 on equality in December 2008 (OIT Américas 2016).

Pay transparency

Pay transparency, including pay that is comparable across a range of gender-related indicators, is essential to inform the content and scope of pay negotiations and collective agreements and in order to promote gender-neutral wage-setting. In recent years, trade unions have given much greater attention to pay transparency in their negotiations. The issue of pay transparency was first raised in the EU in the Danfoss sex discrimination case at the European Court of Justice (ECJ) and was later taken up by the European Parliament (2013). It was established as a key priority in the European Commission's (2010) "Strategy for equality between men and women 2010–2015", leading to agreement for a non-binding "Recommendation on improving pay transparency" (European Commission 2014). The recommendation included an employee's right to request information on gender pay levels for the same work or work of equal value; an employer's duty to report on average gender pay levels by category of employee or position; an employer's duty to conduct an audit on pay and pay differentials on grounds of gender; and measures to ensure that the issue of equal pay, including pay audits, are discussed at the appropriate collective bargaining level.

Coupled with national legislation in some member states (Veldmann 2017), the recommendation on pay transparency has provided a useful, if non-binding, justification for unions calling for pay transparency measures in their pay negotiations. The social partners are viewed as

41

playing a crucial role in the design and implementation of pay transparency (Eurofound 2018). In Austria, Belgium, Denmark, France, Norway and Sweden, legislation provides for pay reporting duties on gender pay differentials at company level. In the Netherlands and Sweden, upon request, equality bodies, and in Sweden, trade unions as well, can have access to the necessary information in cases of a potential pay discrimination claim. In addition, the Swedish National Mediation Office produces a detailed annual report on wage differences between men and women, of vital use in negotiations between the Swedish LO and the Confederation of Swedish Enterprises. The report analyzes trends, taking into account differences in occupation, sector, education, age and working hours, as well as unexplained wage differences. Analysis of the main collective agreements has found higher wage increases negotiated in female-dominated companies compared to those in male-dominated companies (National Mediation Office 2014). However, progress remains slow in many EU member states, leading the European Commission (2017) to conclude that "the lack of visible progress in combating pay discrimination, as well as the persisting gender pay gap and the limited follow-up to the Recommendation suggest a possible need for further targeted measures at EU level" (11).

Pay audits or income reports to identify and address pay gaps at workplace level

In recent years, a number of countries in Europe have introduced or are planning to introduce new gender-differentiated pay reporting obligations, which have been the basis for collective negotiations between unions and employers. Pay audit duties are found in the laws of Finland, France, Iceland, Sweden and the UK and company-level agreements for conducting pay audits or income reports have been negotiated in the public and private sectors in Austria, Denmark, Sweden, Finland, France, Iceland and the UK. In those countries where pay surveys or income reports are required in legislation, it has been easier to conclude collective agreements with employers on equal pay. The textbox below gives a brief overview of these provisions in Austria, Sweden, Iceland, France and the UK.

EUROPE: THE IMPACT OF MANDATORY REPORTING OBLIGATIONS ON THE GENDER PAY GAP

In *Austria*, which has one of the highest gender pay gaps in the EU, a 2011 amendment to the Equal Treatment Act introduced provisions to tackle the gender pay gap and achieve transparency in workplace pay systems through the compilation of income reports. The Austrian Trade Union Federation (ÖGB) and the Chamber of Labour actively participated in the development of these measures. In addition, the Works Constitution Act requires the social partners to address equal opportunities in collective agreements and includes provisions for works councils to establish equal opportunities committees and to conclude agreements at company level. The GPA-djp and Vida trade unions support special rounds of collective bargaining to address the persistently large gender pay gap in Austria.

In *Sweden*, employers must perform a mandatory gender pay survey and report. As amended in January 2017, the Swedish Discrimination Act requires a written pay audit to compare gender pay differences for equal work; female-dominated and other work of equal value and female-dominated and other work better paid but with working requirements deemed lower. The report must be made available to the trade union of the applicable collective agreement and the equality ombudsperson.

A further method has been introduced in the banking and finance sector in Sweden, when the Employers' Association of the Swedish Banking Institutions (BAO) and the Financial Sector Union of Sweden (FSU) agreed to tackle non-objective (or unexplained) pay gaps, during the 2011–14 agreement. This required companies to examine certain groups of employees in jobs considered equal to place an increased responsibility on the pay-setting managers during the pay reviews to rectify non-objective pay gaps. In addition, managers receive statistical support to identify pay rates for women and men prior to the pay talks. A handbook sets out how the method can be applied, with opportunities to adapt the method locally within the framework of the agreement (ETUC 2014).

In *France*, legislation requires companies with 50 or more employees (and in a more detailed form, companies with at least 300 employees) to draw up annually "comparative equality reports" concerning the situation of men and women employees, in terms of qualifications, recruitment, training, pay, working conditions and work–family balance. Pay refers to the average monthly wage per job category (European Commission 2017b).

> In *the UK*, the Equality Act (Gender Pay Gap Information) April 2017 requires companies with more than 250 employees in the private sector to publish annually, both mean and median gender pay gaps including mean bonuses. These pay reports are being used by trade unions to take equal pay cases, for example in the case of supermarket workers.
>
> In *Iceland*, within four years from January 2018, a new law requires private companies with 25 or more employees and government agencies to carry out pay audits and receive certification that equal pay is provided or else face steep fines. The aim is to reduce the gender wage gap that has stayed stubbornly at 16 per cent for many years.
>
> In *Germany* and *Ireland*, the governments have also announced plans to introduce pay transparency measures (European Commission 2017b).

This approach to pay transparency is largely confined to Europe, whereas in other parts of the world, for example, in Australia, New Zealand and Canada, there is greater reliance on tribunals and awards in dealing with pay equity issues. However, there are examples of social partner initiatives in the banking sector, where the National Australia Group and the Finance Sector Union of Australia agreed to undertake a pay audit and carry out further joint work in the area and was subsequently awarded a company decent work award by UNI global union (Parker *et al.* 2011). In New Zealand, the five-year pay equity plan of action (2004–09) remains an example of tripartite good practice. The plan aimed at addressing the gender pay gap and promoting equal pay for work of equal value in the public services. Led by the Department of Labour and supervised by a tripartite steering group, there were regular pay equity reviews and a set of workplace initiatives between the social partners (Parker *et al.* 2011). With the new Labour–New Zealand First–Green Party government in place, a joint working group on pay equity has been reconvened to introduce amendments to the 1972 Equal Pay Act. The aim is to find ways to facilitate equal pay cases, by making it easier to find comparators. The Public Services Alliance (PSA) has welcomed the new approach: "Since the new Labour-led Government was elected, we've been making good progress on the road to equal pay, despite the odd barrier being thrown up in front of us" (PSA National Secretary, Erin Polaczuk, March 2018).

Individualized pay setting and performance-related pay

Across the world in the public and private sectors, there has been a shift towards the individualization of pay setting and the introduction of performance-related pay. Many unions oppose performance-related pay because of the lack of transparency. In some countries, such as Germany and Sweden, some agreements in the public sector eliminate performance-related pay awards altogether. Establishing clear criteria for the award of performance-related pay has become an important issue for trade union negotiations for workers in professional job categories. For example, the Swedish Confederation of Professional Associations (SACO) has bargained to reduce the gender pay gap through a greater focus on transparency in the individualization of wages. A wage search tool designed to promote transparency in performance payments has been developed for university staff. Agreements have sought to provide pay transparency and fair systems to enable individuals to negotiate their wages based on market rates. This is seen as an important way to close the gender pay gap as women are less likely than men to negotiate higher salaries – an issue recently revealed in the UK where some women journalists working in the BBC discovered they were earning almost half the earnings of their male counterparts.

Gender-neutral job classification and job evaluation systems

Some unions have drawn up bargaining strategies that focus on discriminatory job classification schemes and job evaluation free from gender bias, on the basis that equal pay for work of equal value (under the EU Equal Pay Directive and ILO Convention no. 100) presupposes that there are mechanisms in place for comparing the value of jobs using gender-neutral criteria. In Canada (Ontario and Quebec) and New Zealand, for example, collective bargaining for equal pay for work of equal value and gender-neutral job evaluation has been considerably strengthened as a result of national pay equity legislation. However, in other countries, equal pay legislation fails to address equal pay for work of equal value, such as Law 20-348 in Chile adopted in 2009 on the right to equal pay.

Collective agreements on gender-neutral job classifications and job evaluation schemes can address both gender segregation in the classification of jobs and the systematic undervaluing of women's work. Collective agreements in Belgium, France, Sweden and the UK have implemented gender-neutral job evaluation using objective and analytical criteria (using factors of skill, effort, responsibility and working conditions). For example, landmark agreements in the UK (the Single Status Agreement in local government and the Agenda for Change in the health sector) paved the way for gender-neutral evaluation of all jobs and the upgrading of women's pay in jobs that were undervalued, particularly affecting care workers (EPSU 2013). In Cyprus, training has been provided for labour inspectors and the social partners on job evaluation free from gender bias, under an EU-funded project on equal pay implemented by the Department of Labour Relations. In Germany, negotiations and strike action by workers in municipal social and child-care services resulted in an agreement for a new pay and grading system and negotiations commenced in 2014, in order to remove discrimination in the system.

In Belgium legislation on equal pay passed in 2012 introduced the "obligation to negotiate measures to address the wage gap at the sectoral level", and gender neutral job classification is regarded as a good practice example in Europe (European Commission 2016c). The law encourages collective bargaining on the issue, and includes provision of wage data and mandatory action plans in companies with more than 50 employees. Sectoral collective agreements and joint committees are required to draw up gender-neutral and non-discriminatory job classifications. The Institute for the Equality of Women and Men in Belgium drew up a set of guidelines on "Gender neutrality in job evaluation and classification" (Pardon & Baird 2013). Unions drew up additional guidelines in order to prepare negotiators for the implementation of the legislation.

Increasing the value of women's work has also been a key strategy for trade unions in France. In 2004 a job evaluation grid for assessing the equivalence of women's work and men's work was drawn up. The French unions argue that it is important to have objective criteria that address the undervaluing or non-recognition of women's skills (Pillinger 2014). For example, an agreement between the FO trade union and the French electricity company, EDF, on professional equality between women and men for the years 2012–14, includes a chapter on "The pursuit of equal pay" and sets out a system for assessing the job position, skills, seniority, training and professionalism at least once a year. Monitoring is conducted to ensure that the measures are implemented and that part-time workers are treated equally to full-time workers.

LATIN AMERICA: NEW INITIATIVES IN THE PUBLIC SECTOR TO ADDRESS THE GENDER PAY GAP THROUGH INTRODUCING GENDER-NEUTRAL JOB EVALUATION SCHEMES

Since 2002, the PSI has developed a global pay equity campaign and supports its affiliates to advocate for gender-neutral job evaluation systems. In Peru, the Lambayeque water trade union, member of FENTAP national union, collaborated with the Public Water and Sanitation Board (EPSEL SA) to develop a gender-neutral job evaluation scheme. The agreement to undertake the job evaluation was a result of a labour court ruling on a complaint from the union about the highly distorted and arbitrary pay classification system. The labour court required the company and union to review the job classification system. Using the ILO equal pay manual (Oelz *et al.* 2013) and PSI training materials on gender-neutral job evaluation (Green 2008), a bipartite job evaluation task force was set up, with the support of an external consultant, the PSI affiliates' women's committee and the ILO. The task force members were trained in gender-neutral job evaluation techniques and concepts related to equal pay. It was also agreed to carry out an occupational health risk assessment at the plant. The members of the task force then administered a survey based on interviews with 166 of the 800 workers to collect information about the requirements of every job. They then applied a new job classification system based on objective criteria: skills, responsibility, effort and working conditions, and giving value to the work traditionally carried out by women and generally overlooked. Special attention was given in the interviews to any unsafe or unhealthy conditions workers reported. These were referred to the joint health and safety committee for resolution. Over time, the salary scales will be gradually modified so that they are in keeping with the new classification system. Every year, a budget is assigned to pay for these upward adjustments.

A further good example of trade union work to eliminate gender bias in job evaluations can be found in the public sector in Chile. Chile's National Association of Civil Servants (ANEF) has approximately 75,000 affiliates, 58 per cent of members are women, and it is affiliated to the national trade union confederation, CUT, and to the PSI. ANEF's work to promote gender equality is informed by the state's international obligations and the Chilean law 20-348 on equal pay, adopted in 2009. ANEF argued that it is the state's obligation to lead as a good practice employer. The government-ANEF public sector protocol agreement in 2015 includes clauses on the promotion of equal pay. In 2016, a government Treasury study (*Ministerio de Hacienda*) found that the pay gap for the public sector was 10.4 per cent overall and 19.5 per cent in technical posts; and that women were under-represented in management positions. The average pay gap for Chile's entire workforce was 21.1 per cent. The government agreed to set up a bipartite committee to design and implement a new job evaluation system as a pilot scheme for the Social Security Institute (ISL). The values of the posts were calculated jointly between the union, the Association of Employees of ISL and the human resources department of the ISL. The Treasury issued a report on the job classification process; and a new job evaluation instrument is in preparation that can be used across the public sector. The union has said that the whole process has been very participative and has strengthened the level of women's participation in the union:

> When the Chilean law was adopted in 2009, we realised it really addressed only 50 per cent of the problem because it did not mention equal pay for work of equal value, only equal pay. We thought this is a "white elephant" as we didn't have the instruments to measure work of equal value and how to address the issue. We had both the support of the PSI pay equity campaign and the ILO to help us to start the work of measuring the pay gap and designing a new job classification system. We also had a supportive government giving priority to gender equality issues and gender experts and champions in the Treasury and Ministry of Labour.[1]

Several examples of how job evaluation has been used to improve women's pay and streamline pay systems can be found in Africa, including in South Africa and Ghana. The South African public sector adopted the "Equate" job evaluation system for the public service in 1999, following

---

1. Interview by Nora Wintour with Angela Rifo, equal pay coordinator and vice president for international relations, and Carlos Insunza, president of ANEF, 21 February 2018.

an extensive benchmarking review. Job evaluation was mandatory for all new jobs and all higher-level appointments and was drawn up with the intention of addressing serious inequities and discriminatory practices on grounds of race, gender and disability. At the time, it was noted that job evaluation was the main mechanism available to ensure compliance with the principle of equal pay for work of equal value.

More recently, public service job evaluations have been driven by the need to develop mechanisms within the public service salary system to attract and retain critical skills. For example, in Ghana, there was a major job evaluation exercise over a two-year period, involving over 470,000 public sector workers from 80 public institutions. The migration of public sector workers onto the new single spine salary system (SSSS), based on the UK model, took place starting January 2010 and was completed in December 2011. Previously public sector workers had been operating under almost 100 separate salary structures (Wintour 2013). The new SSSS was designed to increase the level of objectivity and transparency in salary classifications and to ensure that the public sector was a profession of choice by including a market or retention premium. The trade unions participated in the job analysis and working sessions and in the negotiations for the retention premium. However, the ILO Committee of Experts on the Application of Conventions and Recommendations (ILO 2009b) has raised concerns about the extent to which the job evaluation took into account the principle of equal pay for work of equal value and it is to be noted that the Ghana Labour Act refers to the "right to equal pay for equal work". None of the current CBAs in the public sector refer to the principle of equal pay for work of equal value.

Despite some progress made in this area in collective bargaining, applying gender-neutral job evaluation schemes has been difficult to implement. Complexity, lack of resources and expertise, the absence of comparators, a lack of wage transparency and decentralized bargaining continue to be major barriers to implementation (Pillinger 2014). In some countries legislation does not refer to prohibition of discriminatory job classification systems or provide a definition of "work of equal value", making it difficult for unions to persuade employers to tackle the issue in collective bargaining.

Minimum/living wage policies

Because women are less likely to be covered by collective agreements, unions have advocated for minimum or "living" wages[2] as an effective mechanism to increase women's wages in both developed economies and emerging and developing economies (ILO 2014a). Research from Belgium, for example, shows that when minimum wages increase, earnings inequality and the gender pay gap decreases (Vandekerckhove 2012). Analysis of the introduction of the national living wage in the UK by the Resolution Foundation (2015) found that women were the main beneficiaries (three in every 10 female workers saw an increase in their pay, compared with fewer than one in five men). Many unions, however, argue that minimum wage policies alone are insufficient to address the structural causes of the pay gap.

Currently, 26 out of 34 OECD countries have statutory minimum wages (OECD 2015). Recent studies have shown that minimum wages – sometimes combined with strengthened collective bargaining – have contributed to reducing inequality in some Latin American countries (Kiefman & Maurizio 2012), as well as in other emerging and developing economies. However, minimum wage policies may exclude some female-dominated sectors, affecting for example domestic workers, garment workers or agricultural workers, or are often set so low as to be meaningless. Minimum wages may also result in entrenching discrimination by setting wages for certain female-dominated sectors or occupations, lower than for others, such as is the case for domestic workers (Hobden 2015; ILO 2016c). In other contexts, such as India and South Africa, there are multiple minimum wage rates and very complicated

---

2. A "minimum wage" (at national, sectoral or regional level) is the minimum amount that the employer is required by law or collective agreement to pay a worker. The amount can be set by the hour or by other periods according to national legislation or collective agreement. A "living wage" is an amount that a trade union, coalition or think tank has calculated based on what a worker really needs to earn to meet the cost of living. In the UK, inspired by the living wage campaign (www.livingwage.org.uk) in April 2016, the government increased the legal minimum wage rate, renaming it, confusingly, the national living wage.

systems, which also limit the extent to which they are effectively enforced (Berg 2015).

In Europe, minimum wage setting takes place in three broad areas: statutory minimum wages determined by legislation; extended minimum wages set through collective agreements for a region, industry or professional group; and collectively agreed minimum wages negotiated with employers based on an employer's minimum ability to pay (mainly in countries with no statutory minimum wage, for example, in the Nordic countries). Increasing minimum wages has the potential to reduce the gender pay gap (Eurofound 2013a; Grimshaw *et al.* 2013; Rubery & Grimshaw 2011). Data from five European countries shows a strong relationship between collective bargaining and the minimum wage. The ETUC "Bargaining for Equality" survey (Pillinger 2014) found that nearly one-third of unions had negotiated collective agreements on minimum wages or pay increases for low-paid workers, with a focus on "living wages". In many cases the pay bargaining strategies of trade unions and employers shape the pay equity effects of minimum wage policy (Grimshaw, Bosch & Rubery 2013). In several countries, including Norway, Germany, Italy and Finland, collective agreements can extend sectoral minimum wages to non-organized enterprises. Countries that collectively agree minimum wages have a smaller low-pay segment and greater protection exists for part-time and temporary workers (Eurofound 2014).

In developing economies, many unions are giving priority to living wage campaigns. For example, IndustriALL adopted a living wage campaign in 2013, with a particular focus on the textile and electronics sectors, on the basis that achieving a sectoral agreement on a living wage would predominantly benefit women at the lower end of the wage scales. It was also recognized that because the majority of union negotiators are men in many Asian countries, a specific gender equality strategy might have less traction. IndustriALL has supported a series of training workshops on the issue of minimum wages and living wages, in Cambodia, Vietnam and Indonesia. In Vietnam, a sectoral agreement, first signed in 2010, and renewed in 2013, has increased minimum wage thresholds. However, despite the strategy to progressively achieve living wages in

Vietnam, in 2018 the tripartite Vietnam National Wage Council only recommended a minimum wage increase of 6.5 per cent, half of what the Vietnam General Confederation of Labour had called for, and representing the lowest increase in 11 years.

Pay increases in female-dominated sectors

Improving the pay of low-paid women workers has had significant impact on reducing the gender pay gap in the public sector (EPSU 2013). Some collective agreements have addressed the problems associated with occupational segregation and the undervaluing of women's work by targeting additional wage increases for workers in female-dominated sectors. Workers in female-dominated sectors are awarded above average pay rises, in order to redress the historic undervaluing of women's work, occupational segregation and in recognition of collective bargaining strategies that historically awarded higher average pay rises to male-dominated sectors.

The ETUC "Bargaining for Equality" survey (Pillinger 2014) found that 26 per cent of respondents negotiated specific wage increases for women in female-dominated sectors. These have been exclusively negotiated by union confederations and have been designed to "raise the floor" by increasing the pay for low-paid workers in the female-dominated sectors and occupations. For example, the Icelandic Confederation of Labour prioritized additional pay increases for low-paid workers in their negotiations for collective agreements both in 2008 and 2010. Additional payments for low-paid workers were negotiated, mainly in female-dominated groups in unskilled or semi-skilled jobs in the health and care sector. During the economic crisis, the Confederation of Labour sought to protect these groups from further pay cuts. In Norway, following pay increases for low-paid workers in the public sector, the Norwegian Gender Equality Commission recommended targeted pay increases for female-dominated occupations in the public sector. In Ireland, MANDATE, the retail workers' trade union negotiated agreements for improved pay and decent work for the predominantly female, low-paid and part-time retail sector (Pillinger 2014).

Other strategies include abolishing the lowest grades in the public sector in Denmark and in local government in the UK, and negotiating flat-rate pay increases for low-paid public sector workers in Germany. In the UK, the wage settlement for local government workers led to the abolition of the lowest pay grades, resulting in a 2.3 per cent increase for workers who moved up to the next grade. In Bulgaria, improvements in the pay of low-paid women in female-dominated jobs were achieved in the health sector (EPSU 2013).

Equality allowances

Use of special funds, or "equality allowances", is another approach taken to address pay inequalities, whereby an additional equality budget is negotiated in a collective agreement. Collective agreements in Finland, Sweden and Norway have targeted workers in female-dominated jobs through equality allowances. In Finland, equality allowances have been negotiated in order to provide higher pay increases in collective agreements – the size of the allowance is dependent on the extent to which jobs are female-dominated or low-paid. In the sectoral agreements for 2012–14, 0.5 per cent of the total wage costs were allocated to reduce pay inequalities between women and men. LO-Sweden and the Swedish employers' organization agreed an equality allowance for female-dominated occupations. The 2013 national agreement specified that in all sectors with average wages lower than SEK 25,000 per month, there would be an increase of a minimum amount instead of a percentage. LO-Sweden considers the introduction of flat-rate increases as another way to reduce the percentage difference between low-paid female-dominated jobs and other male-dominated jobs. In Norway, unions have negotiated higher pay increases for women in female-dominated sectors in the public and private sectors. Norway's State General Collective Agreement has a chapter on local agreements setting out that "where documented salary differences cannot be explained other than by sex, the employer shall, in consultation with the unions, fix wage differences according to the Equality Act".

MATERNITY PROTECTION, PARENTAL LEAVE AND WORK–LIFE BALANCE

In the context of marked improvements in legislation on maternity protection, parental leave and work–life balance over the last two decades, this section examines how collective bargaining has addressed these core equality issues. In countries where there is still employer liability for maternity leave allowances, unions have been advocates for the introduction of social insurance schemes and the extension of such schemes to cover informal workers as well. In countries with national insurance coverage, and with longer leave entitlements, bargaining has also sought to ensure that women on maternity leave have entitlements that are extended beyond the law and do not lose out in terms of career development. In Europe and many OECD countries, parental and paternity leave is well established in legislation and many collective agreements have extended legal entitlements. In Latin America, paternity leave is increasingly common and is incorporated into many union bargaining agendas.

This section also examines how over the last two decades unions, particularly in Europe and other OECD countries, have bargained on work–life balance, and considers how bargaining goals have shifted from the reduction of working hours to employee-oriented flexible working time, designed to promote work/family balance and provide more individual choice. These objectives are also increasingly voiced in collective bargaining claims in Latin America and some Asian countries, as well as in the USA. However, a new and urgent bargaining issue is to address the increasing fragmentation and uncertainty around working hours that makes it increasingly difficult for women and men to reconcile work and family life. This is particularly a consequence of growing levels of precarious work since the economic crisis, including a growth of casual and "zero working hours" contracts.

Strengthened maternity protection legislation

Since the adoption in 2000 of ILO Convention 183 on Maternity Protection and its accompanying Recommendation 191, there have been marked improvements in maternity protection legislation around the world with longer leave entitlements at childbirth, improved paid benefits, with a trend to move away from employer liability towards contributory universal social insurance schemes. In many countries, unions have been at the forefront of campaigns calling for the ratification of ILO Convention 183 and the establishment of national insurance schemes. For example, in the Philippines, in October 2015, maternity leave was extended to 100 days for female employees in both government service and the private sector, with the option for an additional 30 days leave without pay. The unions had been at the forefront of this campaign. Furthermore, women workers in non-standard forms of employment, including domestic workers and urban informal workers, are increasingly benefitting from maternity protection.

Measures safeguarding pregnant women from dismissal and prohibiting discrimination related to pregnancy are integral to maternity protection. In nearly all countries in the world, there is legislation to prohibit dismissal during pregnancy and maternity leave, which is often reflected in CBAs. Interventions to help women return to the workplace after maternity leave are also a significant issue for collective bargaining, especially in female-dominated sectors and workplaces. In some countries, maternity leave is considered a period of service in terms of employment rights. It is less common for legislation to stipulate the right to breast-feeding breaks on return to work (Addati, Cassirer & Gilschrist 2014). However, gaps remain in many developing countries (Stumbitz *et al.* 2017).

In Europe, the European Parliament adopted a revised maternity leave directive in October 2010. It proposed to extend fully-paid maternity leave to 20 weeks, strengthen protection against dismissal for mothers returning to work and provide two weeks fully-paid paternity leave, also for same sex couples. The ETUC noted in support of the proposed revised directive that "pregnancy and maternity security are in fact essential for achieving gender equality and the protection of women's rights". However, it was stalled in the European Council and finally withdrawn in July 2015. This was followed by a European Commission consultation on reconciliation measures and a proposal for a directive on work–life balance for parents and carers (European Commission 2017a), as discussed below.

A notable exception to the trend to extend maternity leave protection is in the USA where the 1993 Family and Medical Leave Act (FMLA) only provides 12 weeks of unpaid leave for the birth or adoption of a child, which is one of the lowest levels of leave in the industrialized world. However, only around 40 per cent of women workers are eligible because of applicability provisions requiring minimum hours of service and the exclusion of companies with less than 50 employees. In 2013, only 12 per cent of private sector workers had access to paid maternity leave and for low-wage earners, the figure was only 5 per cent (Bureau of Labor Statistics 2013). The USA is now one of three countries in the world, in company with Papua New Guinea and Oman, that does not provide paid maternity leave. A 2013 bill was submitted to Congress to create a national paid family and medical leave but was not adopted. However, some states have adopted legislation to provide paid maternity leave (California, New Jersey, New York, Hawaii and Rhode Island) (Addati, Cassirer & Gilschrist 2014). The AFL-CIO and the union movement generally support reforms to the FMLA to expand its coverage and the creation of a paid family and medical leave insurance programme. Collective bargaining, particularly in the public sector, has included provisions for paid maternity leave. For example, in California, unionized employees were more than three-and-a-half times more likely to have access to leave benefits above the legal requirements than non-unionized employees. Unions have also actively pursued pregnancy discrimination claims, particularly practices of job dismissal.

The role of collective bargaining in strengthening maternity protection

Collective bargaining has been an essential tool at national, sectoral and enterprise level to affirm existing legislative provisions and thus strengthen compliance, and to improve upon legal minimum requirements. Bargaining has also sought to ensure that women on maternity leave do not lose out in terms of career development but maintain contact with the workplace, retain service entitlements and participate in relevant training opportunities while on leave.

In Australia, paid maternity leave entitlements were not widespread until the adoption of the 2010 Paid Parental Leave Act although unions actively negotiated for enhanced maternity leave arrangements and protection from discrimination. By 2010, only 14 per cent of agreements included a paid maternity leave (Baird & Murray 2012). Over half of the agreements were in the public sector – a typical duration negotiated for maternity leave was 14–18 weeks in the public sector and 12 weeks in the private sector. Despite progress in this area, differences in duration and provision of maternity leave continue to exist between the public and private sectors. The National Tertiary Education Union (NTEU) achieved improved paid maternity leave from 12 weeks to 26–36 weeks in the early 2000s. Other improvements made at some institutions include access to paid leave for casual employees, pre-natal leave to attend medical appointments, breastfeeding breaks and designated spaces, entitlements to "stay in touch" with the workplace during leave, rights to return to the previous position upon return from leave, and rights to return to work part-time.

Collective agreements have extended the duration of paid maternity leave in Brazil, Paraguay and Colombia. Maternity leave entitlements have been extended through collective bargaining in Argentina and in some cases the company agrees to make up the difference between maternity leave monthly payments from the social security and the worker's regular pay. Some collective agreements also include provisions limiting or prohibiting overtime during pregnancy or during the last few months of pregnancy. In countries where it is not provided for in labour legislation, some collective agreements stipulate leave entitlements in the case of adoption (OIT Américas 2016).

In the education sector almost 60 per cent of unions responding to EI's quadrennial survey (Wintour 2015) consider there have been improvements in maternity protection provisions and parental leave for teachers and education personnel since 2010 and that they had good practice examples through collective bargaining to share. Some improvements relate to an increase in the duration of the maternity leave or improved provisions to facilitate breast-feeding or nursery facilities.

**GOOD PRACTICE EXAMPLE OF PAID MATERNITY LEAVE
NEGOTIATED BY PUBLIC SECTOR UNIONS**

In *South Africa*, in 2010, the Public Service Coordinating Bargaining Council and the Education Labour Relations Council agreed to increase maternity leave to four consecutive months on full pay and an additional leave without pay for 15 months as well as rights to paid leave for prenatal medical examinations and tests; adoption leave, family responsibility leave and urgent private affairs (educators specifically) of 12-working days per annum with full pay – to be reduced if family responsibility leave is taken.

In *Korea*, the KFTA teachers' union negotiated a one-year leave of absence without pay for any male or female employee with a child under 8 years old and this leave is additional to the 90 days paid maternity leave.

Another trend has been the extension of maternity protection to new groups of workers, including contract and agency workers and to informal economy workers. While in some cases, this has been achieved through the introduction of universal social protection schemes or the extension of contributory systems to rural workers or urban informal economy workers, in other cases, it is a result of collective bargaining. For example, in Denmark and Italy, collective bargaining has been used to improve maternity protection for agency workers.

In Asia, unions have advocated for improvements in social insurance schemes. For example, in Sri Lanka, the Lanka Jathika Estate Workers' Union, representing plantation workers, has advocated for the right to maternity leave to be applied uniformly to all women workers, irrespective of sector. Equally, the Free Trade Zone Workers' and General Workers' Union, which represents workers in enterprises operating in EPZs, has submitted proposals to the Minister of Labour for the extension of coverage to women workers employed on time-bound contracts, women in the informal economy, and domestic workers. Both unions have reiterated the need to introduce an insurance scheme to enable maternity benefits to be accessed by all women on maternity leave (Cruz 2012).

In recent years, there is considerable evidence from the ETUC survey and other sources of the curtailment of rights to maternity leave and benefits, women returning from maternity leave and being the first to be made redundant, as well as the difficulties of realizing rights agreed in collective contracts (Pillinger 2014). Many union representatives dedicate considerable time to ensuring that basic maternity entitlements are respected (Stumbitz *et al.* 2017). As the president of the Union of Professionals at BioBio Cement, Curicó, Chile states:

> When a woman is pregnant, there is a need for constant nego-
> tiation. Women feel very insecure when they become preg-
> nant and are unsure how the company will react. Women are
> protected from dismissal for a period of time but when that
> is ended, you never know whether you will continue working.
> More than any other issue, it is maternity rights which we
> need to raise with the company, such as breast-feeding rights,
> different work schedules, taking leave for medical check-ups
> for the child.[3]

In summary, unions have been part of the advocacy to achieve legislation on maternity protection through the ratification of the ILO convention, and collective bargaining has been able to build on existing legal entitlements to maternity leave, improving the duration and benefits available, ensuring that maternity leave is treated as continuous employment, providing paid leave for medical check-ups, reducing working hours during pregnancy and on return to work, the provision of breast-feeding breaks, both in terms of the number of hours per day and the duration, as well as nursery and day care services for infants. In some countries,

---

3. Correspondence with Nora Wintour from Lorena Ibacache, president of the Union of Professionals at BioBio Cement, Curicó, Chile, affiliated to the Federation of Cement Workers of Chile, member of Building and Wood Workers' International, 17 November 2015.

unions have also negotiated additional premiums for the birth of a child, or in case of adoption and miscarriage. Unions have also formed part of wider coalitions to call for reforms in national insurance schemes to end individual employer liability and to extend coverage to women informal workers.

Reconciliation of work and family life

Reconciliation of work and family life is increasingly recognized as fundamental to the realization of gender equality, in turn a reflection of the increased proportion of married women in the workforce with dependent children. In the ETUC "Bargaining for Equality" survey, unions in some countries reported that women's working hours and difficulties in reconciling work and family life were the biggest barriers to gender equality. There is also substantial consensus between the social partners on the crucial role that workplace-level negotiations can play in providing more family-friendly workplaces, as reflected in the ETUC's campaign launched in 2017: "Time to deliver on women's rights: YES to the work–life balance directive".

The European Commission's (2015) "roadmap for reconciliation measures" provided a new opportunity for unions to engage in negotiations around working hours and flexible working time. Following a consultation process, in 2017, the European Commission published a work–life balance package of legal and policy measures to build on existing rights to parental leave, and through a directive to introduce an entitlement to paternity leave, the right to request carer's leave and flexible working arrangements if parents have a child up to 12 years old (European Commission 2017b).

Parental leave

In the European Union, parental leave is well established in national legislation and many collective agreements have extended legal entitlements.

The social partner framework Directive on Parental Leave (Directive 2010/18/EU) includes parental leave for working parents of four months, with the provision to encourage fathers to take leave (whereby at least one of the four months cannot be transferred to the other parent). The leave applies equally in the case of adoption. The European Commission's (2017) proposal for a directive on work–life balance for parents and carers, while extending rights to leave, does not include an obligation to provide paid parental leave, stating that the member states or social partners may define the detailed rules and conditions for such leave. However, there is low take-up of parental leave if it is an unpaid entitlement, particularly so in the case of men (European Commission 2012). For 23 EU member states in 2015, on average only 10 per cent of fathers took parental leave, ranging from 0.02 per cent in Greece to 44 per cent in Sweden. The main reasons for low uptake are related to loss of income, fear of negative impacts on careers, feelings of isolation and prevailing family organization models (Cabrita & Wohlgemuth 2015).

In some cases, unions have negotiated provisions so that parental leave should be taken into account as qualifying periods in pay increases in collective agreements and to encourage the greater take up of parental leave by fathers (Pillinger 2014). Some agreements have also specified that pension contributions should be maintained during parental leave, as is the case for example with agreements in Bulgaria and Denmark. In Luxembourg, a 2005 agreement in the banking sector included provisions for time on parental leave to count as employment when decisions are made about promotion.

**GOOD PRACTICE EXAMPLES ON PAID PARENTAL LEAVE
NEGOTIATED IN COLLECTIVE AGREEMENTS**

The most far-reaching agreement on paid parental leave has been negotiated in *Sweden* by LO-Sweden, based on the argument that if men and women have equal earnings, men would be more likely to take parental leave. The 2013 agreement between LO-Sweden and the Confederation of Swedish Employers led to the introduction of a parental supplement based on a new collectively agreed insurance scheme. The national parental leave insurance compensates for some 80 per cent of the wage reduction up to a certain wage ceiling. This insurance is jointly funded in the form of a fixed premium contributed by all employers covered by the agreement. The agreement effectively doubles the length of time during which employees receive additional payments from the employer on top of state-provided parental leave pay. The unions consider that increasing payments for parental leave will encourage more men to take parental leave.

In *Denmark*, the agreement between the Danish Union of Journalists and the Danish Newspapers' and Media Employers' Association includes provision for journalists who return from parental leave to have the right to an automatic pay rise equal to the average rise of their co-workers. This has been important as one of the barriers to men taking leave is the negative impact on salary levels (European Federation of Journalists, undated).

In the *USA*, unions have actively campaigned for entitlements to parental leave. In December 2015, a new policy was introduced to provide New York City municipal employees with paid parental leave (six weeks of paid time off for maternity, paternity, adoption, and foster care leave, at 100 per cent of salary – or up to 12 weeks total when combined with existing leave).

In *New Zealand*, nearly all collective agreements provide for parental leave, although it is most likely to include extended parental leave without pay. In some agreements, there are clauses to give preferential reappointment to workers after a prolonged absence because of family responsibilities (Parker *et al.* 2011).

In *Latin America*, parental leave is less well established but it is becoming more common for it to be incorporated into collective agreements, for example in Panama where there is no legal provision. In *Argentina*, CONADU, the state university teachers' union, was able to include an innovative clause on parental leave in the national collective contract for public higher education institutions. This allows parents, if they both work in the university sector, to share the leave days in the case of a birth or adoption; however, the mother must take a minimum number of days leave post-partum. In this way, men are also encouraged to participate in the care of their infant during the first months, and it also complies with the legal provisions that recognize same-sex marriage in Argentina.

Work–life balance and working time

Most unions in industrialized countries are actively involved in advocacy and bargaining around work–life balance and working time (Gregory & Miler 2009; ETUC 2011b). Over the last two decades there has also been a shift in the bargaining objective in industrialized countries away from the reduction of working hours to an employee-oriented flexible working time, designed to promote work/family balance and provide more individual choice (ETUC 2011b). While not widespread outside the industrialized world, these objectives are increasingly voiced in collective bargaining, particularly in Latin America and some Asian countries.

The European Commission's (2017) proposal for a directive on work–life balance covers three areas of family-related leave arrangements: parental, paternity and carer's leave; flexible working arrangements; childcare and long-term care. The ETUC's campaign for a strong directive on work–life balance stressed the importance of legislative measures (ETUC 2016). The ETUC argued, however, that the directive should explicitly guarantee the right for autonomous social partners to negotiate and conclude collective agreements on work–life balance according to national law and practice (ETUC 2017a).

Through collective agreements and social partner negotiations, flexible working arrangements to promote parental leave and shared family time have been achieved (ETUC 2006, 2011; Eurofound 2012; Morris & Pillinger 2006; Plantenga & Remery 2006). In some cases, unions have been instrumental in pushing for legal rights to request to work flexible hours (as is the case in Germany, the Netherlands and the UK) and in concluding agreements at national, sectoral and company levels that take account of working time over the life course (Anxo *et al.* 2013; Fagan, Hegewisch & Pillinger 2006). In Australia and New Zealand, collective agreements increasingly include clauses on flexible working time arrangements for employees with children and the right to work part-time (Parker *et al.* 2011).

In the ETUC "Bargaining for Equality" survey, 49 per cent of unions responding to the survey had agreements in the area of reconciliation of work and family life (Pillinger 2014). They cover two broad areas. First, there are agreements that regulate working hours, flexibility in working time, rights of part-time workers and rights for workers with parental responsibilities to increase or decrease their working time and leave arrangements for parents, including additional rights for fathers to enable them to participate in family life. Second, there are agreements that have been instrumental in extending rights to reconciliation, for example, under parental leave or maternity arrangements, beyond the provisions that exist in national legislation.

GOOD PRACTICE EXAMPLES OF COLLECTIVE BARGAINING PROVISIONS TO PROMOTE WORK–LIFE BALANCE

The cross-industry tripartite dialogue in *Germany*, leading to a "charter for family-friendly working hours" provides options for part-time work and family-friendly working hours including for executive positions. In a survey carried out by the union, IG Metall, two-thirds of works' councils considered that this was an important issue, although only 15 per cent of agreements concluded by works' councils contained measures on reconciliation. In 2013, the IG Metall–agreements extended parental leave across the metal and electronic industries (Knüttel 2013). IG Metall gave priority to reconciliation of work and family life as an objective for the 2015 negotiations. In 2018 IG Metall negotiated a major agreement for a 28-hour week – or six hours a day – in their fight for a better work–life balance. The agreement includes a 4.3 per cent pay rise from April 2018, plus much greater flexibility including reduced working time to 28 hours for those who want or need it, and a choice for workers (with children still in education or caring for dependent parents) of an additional pay rise in 2019 or extra paid days off. The agreement covers 900,000 metalworkers, although it is very likely that it will be applied to 3.9 million workers across Germany, with a potential further impact in other industries (ETUC 2018; ETUI 2018). According to a union spokesperson:

> We want employers to recognize that traditional gender roles in modern families are changing, and we want workers to have the chance to do work that is important to society … In the past, demands for more flexibility has come at the cost of workers. We want to flick a switch so that flexible working also benefits workers.[4]

In *Italy*, the confederations have negotiated a number of successful agreements with large companies such as ENEL, Nestlé/San Pellegrino and Bitron. The "Marche region memorandum of understanding" is an innovative approach to facilitate the reconciliation of work and family life, signed in

---

4. Quoted in *The Guardian*, "German workers strike for right to two-year, 28-hour working week", 8 January 2018. Available at https://www.theguardian.com/ world/2018/jan/08/german-metal-workers-strike-in-bid-to-gain-28-hour-w orking-weeks (accessed 24 September 2018).

2014 between the five main unions, ANCI, UPI, CGIL, CISL, UIL, and the main employers' associations. It was premised on the need to promote the sharing of family responsibilities between men and women through second-level collective agreements, with a particular focus on flexible work schedules and work organization. The unions consider that such agreements are essential to promoting women's access to employment. The chemical, textile, energy and manufacturing union, FILCTEM has promoted a "social gender equality model" in second-level bargaining. Practical tools and checklists for companies have been drawn up on how to integrate gender considerations and reconciliation measures into agreements. The union believes that gender equality can only be achieved if negotiators take account of the broader social context of women's public and private lives. Issues include childcare, maternity benefits, flexible working time, part-time work and work shifts, teleworking and training for women returning from maternity leave. In some large companies, additional family and welfare measures have been negotiated in areas such as childcare and support for families with care responsibilities for older people. This has been particularly important in the textile sector where 62 per cent of workers are women (Pillinger 2014).

In the *USA*, many unions have negotiated innovative agreements on work/family balance. AFL-CIO, for example, has a range of resources including bargaining fact sheets providing tips and techniques on bargaining for work/family balance, paid family leave, as well as other issues.

In *Australia*, unions have successfully negotiated agreements on work–life balance, particularly in the public sector, where opportunities to bargain resulted from a combination of public policy development and women's union leadership (Parker *et al.* 2011; Williamson 2009, 2012; Williamson & Baird 2014).

In *New Zealand*, a 2008 survey found that 38 per cent of all collective agreements contained provisions for parental leave without pay, 16 per cent on flexible working hours and only 3 per cent on the right to work part-time (Parker *et al.* 2011).

Predictable working hours

An emerging bargaining issue concerns certainty of working hours, a reflection of the increasing fragmentation and precarious nature of work, particularly as the practice of zero working hours' contracts has spread. Casual and part-time work is more likely to be found in industries and occupations in which women workers predominate. Many workers do not have the job security, or predictability of income and working hours which are so crucial to managing household budgets and organizing family responsibilities.

Women and young workers are disproportionally affected by zero hours' contracts as they are used in retail and other female-dominated sectors. The ETUC has been disappointed at the European Commission's failure to strengthen provisions on secure work in the proposed directive on transparent and predictable working conditions. However, there have been some successful outcomes, largely due to union advocacy and negative public opinion. At the end of April 2017, McDonald's announced it will offer fixed contracts with a minimum number of guaranteed hours every week to some 115,000 UK workers on zero-hours contracts. The change from zero-hours to fixed contracts comes after months of campaigning by the UK union, BFAWU. In New Zealand, innovative collective agreements concluded in 2015 between Unite union and various fast-food chains have eliminated zero hours' contracts and introduced secure and regular shifts.[5]

GENDER-BASED VIOLENCE IN THE WORKPLACE

Gender-based violence is found in every workplace, in every sector of the economy and in every country across the world. Data from the World Health Organization (WHO), based on available country surveys estimates that a shocking 75 per cent of the world's 2.7 billion women aged 18 years and older – at least 2 billion women – have been sexually harassed. WHO also reports that 35 per cent of women (approximately 930 million women), have experienced physical and/or sexual intimate partner violence or non-partner sexual violence in their lifetime. WHO considers this level of violence against women a major public health

---

5. "Zero-hour contracts banned in New Zealand", *The Guardian*, 11 March 2016. Available at: https://www.theguardian.com/world/2016/mar/11/zero-hour-contracts-banned-in-new-zealand

problem as well as a serious violation of the human rights of women (WHO 2017). Some groups of workers, particularly women, are disproportionately affected by violence at work, where unequal power relations, low pay, precarious working conditions and other workplace abuses expose them to violence (Cruz & Klinger 2001; Eurofound 2015a; ILO 2018a). They include informal and casual workers, and workers affected by multiple discrimination, including its worst forms such as debt bondage, trafficking and modern-day forms of slavery (Pillinger 2017b).

The ILO's definition of the "world of work" (Cruz & Klinger 2011; ILO 2018a, 2018b) has been helpful in raising awareness and understanding of the connections between women's care responsibilities and their rights at work as it takes into account travel to and from work, women's safety in public spaces and in employer-provided accommodation, which traditionally have been excluded from the definition of the scope of the workplace.

Trade unions in many countries across the world have carried out negotiations to include violence and harassment in collective agreements and workplace policies, as well as carrying out campaigns and awareness-raising about the importance of negotiations on this issue. Collective bargaining has been considerably strengthened when legislation provides a framework for collective negotiations, including obligations for joint worker–employer initiatives in the workplace, in the framework of occupational safety and health (Pillinger 2017a, 2017b).

Many initiatives have been championed by women's sections within trade unions and, as a result of sustained advocacy, have now been incorporated into the mainstream of union–employer negotiations. The ETUC's "Safe at Home, Safe at Work" study of ten European countries (Pillinger 2017a) cited over 80 examples of collective agreements, and numerous examples of union awareness raising, training and campaigning to address gender-based violence at work, highlighting the importance of a specific gender focus to tackle violence and harassment against women, linked to wider structural gender inequalities. Furthermore, women in unions have used mainstream collective bargaining to challenge unequal gender relations, often in very innovative ways. For example, SACCAWU in South Africa has successfully included the rights of their members to a safe work environment free of gender-based violence, by including it as an issue in company wellness and HIV/AIDS policies and programmes (Lopes & Mapker 2016).

In the education sector, EI research on sexual harassment and gender-based violence in higher education institutions (HEIs) found that both staff and students considered it to be widespread but under-reported (ILO 2018). Sexual harassment is most prevalent in national education systems with low levels of accountability, high levels of poverty and gender inequality, and in institutions that are poorly resourced, where academics are poorly paid and there is a reliance on temporary contracts. Reporting is low as many women fear victimization. There is widespread use of confidentiality clauses and non-disclosure agreements to enable alleged perpetrators to protect their careers, creating a culture of silence where women, and in some cases men, are afraid to make complaints. In the UK, the UCU considers that the growing levels of casual employment in the higher education sector makes women more vulnerable to violence and sexual harassment. The UCU has worked on the issue with the National Union of Students (NUS) and has drawn up a training course for union representatives on how to deal with sexual harassment in the workplace. This is particularly important in male-dominated sectors and union branches. In the school sector, EI has developed an initiative on "School-Related Gender-Based Violence" (SRGBV).[6] Unions are carrying out awareness raising and training in the workplace and lobbying ministries for better resources for prevention.

Women in unions have negotiated agreements on sexual harassment after many years of campaigning and advocacy. In Italy, one landmark agreement in the woodworking sector was the result of advocacy by a women negotiator supported by an active women's network. The agreement gives detailed definitions and procedures for preventing and addressing sexual harassment at work (Pillinger 2017a). Since it was signed, unions have been prioritizing work to implement territorial and company-level agreements, and to engage in dialogue with companies.

---

6. EI/UNGEI/Gender at Work Project, "Education Unions Take Action to Stop School-Related Gender-Based Violence" (SRGBV).

In Denmark, a general collective bargaining was signed in 2008 by the two employers' unions (Local Government Denmark and Danish Regions) and the Danish Association of Local Government Employees' Organizations. It contained a new agreement on preventing, identifying and managing harassment and violence, including sexual harassment and third-party violence at work, and specified that workplace code-termination committees in each region/municipality should draw up guidelines on how to prevent harassment and violence by April 2010 (Local Government Denmark, Danish Regions & KTO 2010) The agreement signed between the French banking group BNP Paribas and the banking union SNB/CFE-CGC (2014) is a particularly good example of a stand-alone agreement on preventing harassment and violence at work, with a strong focus on gender-based violence.

In Spain, unions have adopted a range of strategies to prevent and tackle violence and harassment at work, including the negotiation of CBAs, sexual harassment protocols and gender equality plans in the workplace, much of which has been made possible because of the provisions contained in the Organic Law 3/2007 on gender equality in the workplace. Consequently, gender-based violence at work has been included in many workplace equality plans in companies with more than 250 workers. CBAs and equality plans frequently include reference to the need to raise awareness about sexual and gender-based harassment, including training for management, workers' representatives, and health and safety delegates, among others, as Table 3.2 shows. However, as Alba Garcia, women's secretary, CCOO, Catalonia states, these issues are

Table 3.2: Analysis of 266 sectoral agreements with clauses on sexual harassment in Spain

Type of clause	No. of sectoral agreements	Percentage of sectoral agreements
Prevention of Sexual harassment	207	77.8
Disciplinary measures against perpetrators of sexual harassment	183	68.8

Source: CCOO 2014.

often made worse by the current economic context: "Economic pressure, job insecurity, the dismantling of the welfare state, the impact of poverty and the growing risk of social exclusion are the ideal framework for situations of sexual harassment or violence against women – psychological, physical, economic and sexual" (CCOO 2014: 10).

Increasingly, collective agreements and workplace policies on occupational safety and health include violence and harassment as occupational risks to be tackled through prevention programmes (EU-OSHA 2011; ILO 2016d, 2016e). In this way, violence and harassment at work is approached as a core health and safety or wellbeing at work issue, taking into account the psychosocial risks faced by all workers, not only women. The 2007 European framework agreement on harassment and violence at work (BusinessEurope, ETUC, CEEP & UEAPME 2007) is an example of this more inclusive approach. The agreement has led to the introduction of a substantial number of national and sectoral-level agreements, as well as legislation, to protect workers from violence, including harassment and sexual harassment (BusinessEurope, ETUC, CEEP & UEAPME 2011).

EXAMPLES OF HOW THE LAW HAS STRENGTHENED UNION BARGAINING BY LINKING OCCUPATIONAL SAFETY AND HEALTH TO VIOLENCE AND HARASSMENT AGAINST WOMEN

In *Belgium*, violence and harassment, including sexual harassment, are mainly viewed as psychosocial risks in the workplace under the 2014 Act on Wellbeing at Work, requiring action by workplace safety committees, usually made up of representatives of trade unions and employers. Within this perspective, stress, psychological harassment and sexual harassment at work are issues over which the employer has some control, in terms of work organization, content and environment. In both Belgium and the Netherlands, legislation provides for the appointment of workplace "persons of confidence" who ensure confidential support to victims of violence.

In *Slovenia*, the introduction of the 2009 decree on measures to protect workers' dignity at work in state administration led to the appointment and training of workplace counsellors. The Ministry of Labour, Family, Social Affairs and Equal Opportunities has trained workplace counsellors and the head of each public administration service is required to publicize the role of the counsellors. Good practices have been established in the police and army; these are sectors where complaints of sexual harassment have been made in the past.

In *South Africa*, in the agricultural sector, unions have stressed the importance of safety and health representatives understanding the causes, consequences and ways of preventing violence and harassment at work, including through an intersectional approach. An innovative programme to train occupational safety and health representatives to have a role in violence prevention in farms and factories has been implemented by trade unions, as part of a project supported by the global union IUF, representatives of the Labour Ministry and some employers' organizations. The project has contributed to the training of regional safety and health representatives who have been given access to the farms and workplaces. Despite the success of the programme, women workers' precarious working conditions and lack of job security still make it difficult for victims to come forward and make complaints (Pillinger 2017b).

Unite in *the UK* has appointed bullying and harassment advisors and drawn up guidance for safety reps on how to deal with harassment, bullying and discrimination as an occupational safety and health issue. It has developed a model workplace policy on bullying and harassment at work and a checklist of what safety reps can do to address harassment or violence in the workplace.

The legal framework on sexual harassment in the workplace, as recently introduced in India, Bangladesh, Pakistan and Nepal, requires the establishment of anti-harassment complaints committees. Some unions have started training workplace representatives to sit on these committees (Fair Wear Foundation 2018a).

Some unions have also addressed violence from an intersectional perspective, by focusing on the risks faced by migrant women workers, black and minority ethnic and indigenous women, and LGBTI workers. PSI and EI convene a regular LGBTI forum in order to review union policies. The most recent forum was held in 2017 with a focus on violence and harassment against LGBTI people in the workplace (PSI-EI 2017). The Spanish union CCOO (CCOO 2016b) has adopted a specific protocol for action against sexual harassment and harassment on grounds of sexual orientation, gender identity and/or gender expression. The objective is to achieve an inclusive work environment that allows LGTBI people to be open about their sexuality without fear of discrimination and harassment. A range of bargaining measures are proposed to prevent harassment on the grounds of sexual orientation, gender identity or the expression of gender, including negotiating dedicated procedures and protocols, raising awareness and providing support to LGBTI workers.

A UK audit of trade union action on equality found that half of UK unions had up-to-date materials on bargaining issues related to LGBT workers (TUC 2016). Some unions have also focused on racialized forms of violence and harassment at work (Okechukwu 2014) noting that higher rates of harassment affecting immigrant and racialized workers is also a reflection of their over-representation in high-risk and insecure occupations, for example, in health, education and social services, as shown in research by Canadian union CUPE (2014). Unions have also drawn attention to new and emerging risks in the workplace, and the resulting bargaining challenges, from new forms of work organization and new technology that blurs the lines between workplaces and the home, as well as increased technology-induced surveillance and harassment by employers (ILO 2018b; Moore 2018).

A further issue is finding ways to implement agreements and policies. In Denmark, unions found that existing agreements and workplace policies were insufficient to guarantee violence-free workplaces and they have largely failed to increase reporting and sanctions against perpetrators of sexual harassment. There are multiple reasons for this, including a lack of trust in complaints procedures. In 2016, four Danish trade unions (3F, HK, Serviceforbundet Teknisk Landsforbund and Fængselsforbundet 2016; Pillinger 2017a) set up a task force to implement an integrated strategy to raise awareness of the issue and increase the number of cases taken to litigation, including to the ECJ. The unions also held discussions with politicians regarding the possibility of placing a positive duty on employers to engage in proactive measures to prevent sexual harassment. Unions argued that it is necessary for the employer to be made responsible, especially if the employer had not tried to prevent sexual harassment. The task force developed a media strategy and linked to a Facebook campaign, "Over Stregen" or "crossing the line".

EXAMPLES OF SOCIAL DIALOGUE AND COLLECTIVE BARGAINING TO TACKLE GENDER-BASED VIOLENCE IN THE WORKPLACE

In *Morocco*, women farm workers, supported by a partnership between the US Solidarity Center and the Democratic Labour Federation, have been trained to address gender-based violence. Over 1,000 agricultural workers on five large farms won a landmark contract in 2015 that increased wages, provided safety equipment and other fundamental protections. Since then, union leaders have negotiated an extension of the contract to 200 additional workers at another large farm, Les Domaines Brahim Zniber. New provisions include the first-ever maternity leave, as well as pensions and healthcare. Improvements in working conditions reduce the risk of violence and harassment at work (Pillinger 2018).

The Fair Wear Foundation, a multi-stakeholder initiative with union involvement, works with brands to improve workers' rights in the garment supply chain and has a programme on gender-based violence in the workplace aimed at building social dialogue and implementing workplace policies and programmes (Fair Wear Foundation 2018a, 2018b). Particular focus is given to social dialogue in addressing key supply chain factors that contribute to gender-based violence, including production pressures, enforced overtime and long working hours (Fair Wear Foundation 2018b). Also in the garment sector, the Better Work programme – a partnership between the ILO and the World Bank's International Finance Corporation (IFC) – found that social dialogue, the development of workplace policies, improving factory awareness and carrying out training to reduce sexual harassment have benefitted workers (by reducing levels of sexual harassment), and factory managers (by improving productivity and business performance) (Brown *et al.* 2014; Better Work 2015).

In the cut flower export sector in *East Africa*, collective bargaining has been used to reduce sexual harassment against women, where women make up 70 per cent of the workforce and frequently experience low pay and sexual harassment, including rape (Staritz & Guilherme Reis 2013). In *Uganda*, advocacy by trade unions and NGOs has included the development of policies and confidential complaints procedures to deal with sexual harassment on farms (Evers *et al.* 2014).

Third-party violence and harassment

A relatively new issue concerns third-party violence and harassment at work from customers and clients. Unions report an increase in third-party violence and harassment in front-line and customer facing services such as health and social care, transport, education, catering, hotels and bars, and retail. This issue is rarely addressed in legislation. Reasons for the increase in third-party violence cited by unions include new forms of work organization, work pressures, unrealistic work targets, staffing shortages and stress at work, coupled with growing levels of technology-based workplace surveillance and performance monitoring. Third-party violence is highlighted as a growing problem in services where there is customer/client contact.

Workers in the health sector are at increased risk of violence and harassment at work, as documented in joint research and guidelines drawn up by, PSI, the ILO, ICN and WHO (2002). Incidents of verbal aggression, physical violence and sexual harassment from patients and visitors have grown significantly in recent years (PSI 2018). Public service and education unions cite inadequate funding, leading to increasing levels of violence and harassment at work (EPSU-UNI 2009; EPSU *et al.* 2013a, 2013b; ETUCE 2010; ETUCE-EFEE 2012; PSI 2018). These risks are higher in the public sector and when workers care for vulnerable adults in residential settings.

The Canadian public service union CUPE argues that workplace violence and harassment, a symptom of staffing shortages, has now become the highest concern of workers, leading to new collective bargaining claims to address the issue (CUPE 2018). CUPE's research (2014) found that 38 per cent of long-term care workers experience physical violence daily. A campaign "Time to Care" aimed to raise awareness of the need to increase funding and to legislate for a minimum standard of four hours care per resident per day, with additional resources for the care of older people with complex health problems (CUPE 2017). Migrant health and social care workers may also be in vulnerable work situations if their work permits tie them to a particular employer or where they risk facing unethical forms of recruitment. In disaster management and conflict situations, health workers are often the targets of violence. In PSI's work in the Democratic Republic of Congo, collective agreements in the hospital sector were instrumental in addressing significant levels of violence against healthcare staff (PSI 2018).

In Europe, social partners from the commerce, private security, local government, health and education sectors drew up "multi-sectoral guidelines to tackle third-party violence and harassment at the workplace", signed in July 2010 by European social partners in the services sector (EPSU, UNI Europa, ETUCE, HOSPEEM, CEMR, EFEE, EuroCommerce, CoESS 2013a, 2013b). European education unions also issued guidance on how to reduce and prevent third-party violence and harassment against teachers (ETUCE-EFEE 2012).

In the hospitality sector, there have been recent innovative campaigns. Nordic unions have drawn attention to sexual harassment in the hotel, restaurant and tourism industry (HRCT 2015). The research highlights the importance of the social partners in addressing endemic sexual harassment in the sector. A 2016 survey by UNITE revealed the widespread nature of sexual harassment and abuse by hotel guests. For example, 49 per cent of housekeepers in the survey stated guest(s) had exposed themselves, or answered the door naked. The union used the women's testimonies to persuade male union leaders to support the campaign. This resulted in the union campaign "Hands off, pants on", which led to the City of Chicago passing legislation in 2017 requiring hotel employers to provide housekeeping staff with panic buttons, to protect hotel workers from retaliation when they report sexual violence by guests and to implement anti-sexual harassment policies. The IUF HRCT group has also adopted guidelines to protect the safety of women workers.

Contract cleaning, which often takes place early in the morning or late at night, is another sector where there has been recent union engagement to stop sexual harassment, for example, through the *Ya Basta!* (Enough is Enough!) coalition in California (Yeung 2017). As part of an innovative campaign, involving low-paid migrant workers, women janitors were trained to assist other women who had been sexually harassed at work. Despite some initial resistance from men, sexual harassment and assault became a core union issue. The new contract between the union and the largest cleaning companies in the state includes new provisions and procedures on the prevention of sexual harassment. Core to the success of the campaign was the coalition of workers' rights and anti-sexual violence organizations who created the *Ya Basta!* coalition.

The European Transport Federation (ETF) highlighted the risks of sexual harassment and violence when women work alone or in isolated work situations. The organization noted a significant increase in sexual harassment and other forms of violence against women workers in transport in all European countries (ETF 2017). ETF's (2017) survey on violence against women was used as a basis for engaging transport employers in the EU transport social dialogue committees to give greater priority to tackling violence against women from third-parties and from within the workplace itself (see Chapter 5). The International Transport Federation (ITF) produced an "Action guide on violence against women in transport" (ITF undated) and adopted an informal transport workers' charter (2016), with a section on the rights of women calling for an end to employment discrimination and an end to violence and sexual harassment (ITF 2016).

Domestic violence at work

Unions and feminists have contributed to the conceptual understanding of the employment relationship and how women's wider inequalities and domestic work impact on both women's participation and advancement in work. Campaigning over many years by women in unions and in domestic violence organizations has led to recognition in many unions that domestic violence is a workplace and an occupational health and safety issue (Aeberhard-Hodges & McFerran 2017; Baird, McFerran & Wright 2014; MacGregor, Wathen & MacQuarrie 2017; McFerran 2016; Pillinger 2017a). In this context, domestic violence is regarded as a form of violence that impacts on the workplace and that employers have a "duty of care" to ensure that victims are supported and protected.

Workplace surveys on domestic violence in Australia, Belgium, Canada, Mongolia, New Zealand, Philippines, Taiwan, Turkey and the

UK[7] reveal that on average one-third of workers experience domestic violence at some point in their lives. Around half of victims consider their job performance was negatively affected, resulting in disrupted work histories, high rates of absenteeism, lower personal incomes, and increased resort to casual and part-time work (TUC 2014a). In extreme cases, the workplace can be a place of assault, psychological control and death perpetrated by partners and ex-partners (TUC 2014a; Wathen, MacGregor & MacQuarrie 2015). According to the US Bureau of Labor Statistics (2016) homicide is one of the main causes of workplace deaths for women, accounting for 19 per cent of cases of homicide at work in 2014. When women are murdered at work, it is most frequently by an intimate partner.

The prevention of domestic violence, and its "spill-over" into the workplace are new and potentially transformative areas of bargaining that have galvanized unions in several countries. Recently, debates and campaigns led by global and national trade unions recognize the impact of a wider societal culture of patriarchy and unequal gender relations on the workplace. Research on domestic violence in the workplace shows the devastating impact on victims, including repeated violent assaults at the workplace, stalking, and forms of coercive physical and economic control that may prevent women from getting to work or participating fully in the workplace, and sometimes forcing women to leave the workplace altogether (Makowski *et al.* 2013; McFerron 2011; TUC 2014a; Wathen, MacGregor & MacQuarrie 2014).

ETUC's study "Safe at Home, Safe at Work" (Pillinger 2017a) found universal support among trade unions for future national trade union and ETUC bargaining priorities to include domestic violence at work, on the basis that without paid work, and possibilities for autonomy and financial independence, woman may become economically trapped in a violent relationship. Although a relatively recent bargaining issue, in many European countries an increasing number of trade unions and some employers recognize the role of the workplace in preventing domestic

---

7. For further information about the surveys, see http://dvatworknet.org/research/national-surveys (accessed 24 September 2018).

violence, and the social and economic benefits that result from this. The report cited over 40 examples of collective bargaining agreements and union-negotiated workplace policies on tackling domestic violence at work, as well as awareness raising, training and campaigns carried out by unions, often in partnership with domestic violence organizations.

ETUC "SAFE AT HOME, SAFE AT WORK": TEN THINGS THAT THE ETUC AND ETUC AFFILIATES CAN DO TO TACKLE GENDER-BASED VIOLENCE AND HARASSMENT AT WORK

1. Prioritize sectoral and company-based social dialogue between unions and employers, jointly agreeing workplace policies, procedures and awareness-raising actions for managers and workers.
2. Ensure that women are in senior negotiating positions, as critical to ensuring issues of gender-based violence and harassment are included in bargaining agendas, particularly in male-dominated sectors.
3. Produce guidance and model workplace policies and train workplace representatives to negotiate agreements and policies to tackle violence and sexual harassment at work, third-party violence, and the prevention of domestic violence at work.
4. Ensure that safety and health and well-being at work initiatives include a strong gender-based focus on the causes of and solutions to harassment and violence against women at work and that they take into account gender inequalities and discrimination.
5. Provide information and support to workers experiencing gender-based violence and harassment and domestic violence.
6. Work in partnership with NGOs and specialist violence against women organizations, for example in carrying out campaigns and union surveys to raise awareness about the extent and nature of gender-based violence at work.
7. Encourage women and men in leadership, negotiating and decision-making positions to raise public awareness and act as champions for a zero-tolerance approach to violence against women.
8. Highlight the economic and social case for tackling violence at work, including the business arguments such as improving workplace relations, enhancing well-being at work, retaining workers, reducing absence from work, and increasing motivation and productivity.
9. Lobby for the inclusion of effective measures to address gender-based violence at work and domestic violence at work in governments' national

action plans on violence against women, as well as in the implementation of the 2014 Council of Europe convention on preventing and
combating violence against women and domestic violence (the Istanbul
Convention) and the proposed ILO instrument on violence against
women and men in the world of work.

10. Implement measures to include and address gender-based violence and
harassment in European sectoral social dialogue agreements and joint
statements.

(Source: Pillinger 2017a)

As with other gender-related bargaining issues, there is a strong
business case for employers to bargain on this issue, particularly as
the costs of introducing workplace programmes have been found to
be relatively inexpensive. The costs of domestic violence in the workplace are reduced if employers introduce policies, and safety and support measures, designed to retain women in the workplace. Research
from the European Institute of Gender Equality (EIGE 2014), the UK
(Walby 2004, 2008), the Canadian Federal Justice Department (Zhang *et
al*. 2012) and from Australia, (National Retail Association 2016) put the
costs to employers at millions of dollars every year. The UN Commission
on the Status of Women (2013) estimated the costs could range from
between $1.16 billion to $32.9 billion.

Trade unions are increasingly active in identifying and preventing
situations of risk faced by victims of domestic violence in the workplace. Recent collective bargaining gains on domestic violence at work
have been described as an "equality bargaining breakthrough" (Baird,
McFerran & Wright 2014). The ILO (2018a) recognized domestic violence at work as an issue for a new international labour standard on violence and harassment against women and men in the world of work, in
large measure due to the advocacy and campaigning of women in unions
(Aeberhard-Hodges & McFerran 2017). Vicky Smallman eloquently set
out the role and scope of the workplace in preventing domestic violence from the Canadian Labour Congress (CLC), speaking on behalf
of the worker's group at the ILO Meeting of Experts on Violence against
Women and Men in the World of Work in 2016. She stated that:

Unions are not suggesting that workplaces can take the place of governments and community services, but the workplace is a key part of an integrated approach. Our experience has shown that workplaces can play a vital role in recognizing and responding to domestic violence at work, interrupting the isolation that fuels the abuse, providing support so workers can keep their job, and ensuring a safety plan is in place for the worker and others in the workplace. Where employers and workplaces are unprepared, experience has shown that aggression escalates, even to the point of death, including homicide/suicide at work. Prominent and tragic cases have led to advances in collective bargaining and legislation in different parts of Canada. Prevention, then, comes in the form of early intervention, workplace safety and supports. (cited in Pillinger 2017b)

Legal frameworks can facilitate bargaining for workplace measures on domestic violence. The Istanbul Convention is not explicit on the role of the social partners in the workplace. However, it opens up discussions about the role that the workplace can play in preventing domestic violence. Several EU governments, employers' organizations and unions are exploring how this can be framed in relation to the workplace (CARVE 2016), including under the European company network on preventing domestic violence at work (CEASE Project).[8]

Some countries have begun implementing laws and policies on domestic violence at work, as for example, in Argentina, France, Italy, the Philippines, Spain, Canada, New Zealand and the USA, either using specific laws on domestic violence or gender equality laws, labour laws and codes or occupational safety and health law (Pillinger 2018). The most comprehensive national legal framework can be found in Spain, under Organic Law 1/2004 (28 December 2004) on protection against domestic violence. Trade unions are seeking to reform this law to make it easier for victims to organize their working hours or to obtain a job

---

8. See https://cease-project.eu/ (accessed 24 September).

transfer. The Spanish "National Strategy for the Eradication of Violence against Women" (2013–16) is a comprehensive framework providing guidance and recommendations for companies, employers and trade unions on domestic violence at work policies. Unions in Spain have ensured that the majority of CBAs, harassment and violence protocols and gender equality plans have provisions in place regarding domestic violence. Some agreements and gender equality plans have improved on existing legal measures and most agreements provide information about specialist services, as well as social and psychological support to domestic violence victims. Clauses range from informing domestic violence victims of their rights, preventing domestic violence through training, reorganization of the working day by offering flexible working hours, paid and unpaid leave and a range of other social or economic measures. The Spanish CCOO union's analysis of 266 sectoral agreements found that of 110 agreements containing measures on domestic violence at work, 75.4 per cent defined specific measures such as paid leave of absence and 20.9 per cent introduced new measures, beyond those provided for in the law (CCOO 2014). Despite a strong enabling legal framework, Spanish unions argue that the economic crisis has undermined unions' capacity to negotiate on these issues.

In Italy, following many years of coordinated lobbying by unions and the women's movement, the 2016 Jobs Act enshrines the right to three months paid leave for women victims of domestic violence where a protection order is in place. This new law is regarded as ground breaking by unions, because it treats such leave entitlements as similar to other leave such as maternity leave. Unions in all sectors are examining the implications of the legislation and how domestic violence leave provisions can be negotiated, and where possible extended, in CBAs. As one woman trade unionist said:

> We have had a continuous dialogue about violence against women ... For a long time we have been saying that domestic violence is not the only type of violence and that there is also violence at work. The message eventually got through. (Loredana Taddei, national officer responsible for gender equality, CGIL, Italy; cited in Pillinger 2017a)

Global action and lobbying by unions and NGOs to eliminate and prevent all forms of violence against women and girls, led to the adoption by the 2013 57th session of the UN Commission on the Status of Women (UNCSW57) of recognition of unions as legitimate stakeholders in addressing discrimination, exploitation and violence in the workplace. This was an important breakthrough providing that governments have a responsibility to introduce comprehensive measures to ensure workplaces are free from discrimination, violence and sexual harassment, "in collaboration with employers, unions and workers" (UN 2013). A further development, spearheaded by the union movements, is the draft new International Labour Standard on "violence and harassment against women and men in the world of work", which recognizes the important role for collective bargaining in ensuring that workplaces are free from all forms of violence and harassment, including gender-based violence (ILO 2018a, 2018b).

COLLECTIVE BARGAINING ON DOMESTIC VIOLENCE AT WORK IN THE UK, AUSTRALIA AND CANADA

The journey to establish domestic violence as a workplace issue began in *the UK* when the public service union UNISON negotiated guidelines, a model clause and workplace policy as set out in the 1999 publication *Raise the Roof on Domestic Abuse: A UNISON Guide to Campaigning Against Domestic Violence.* Updated guidance (2015) sets out information about domestic abuse and why it is a trade union issue. UNISON is monitoring how many workplace policies have been drawn up. Following on, the Local Government Association and NHS employers, two of the largest public sector employers, have drawn up domestic violence at work policies. Other unions, including the STUC, the PCS and USDAW have drawn up guidance on domestic violence at work as a basis for negotiations with employers (Pillinger 2017a).

Australia is the first country in the world "to enshrine family and domestic violence leave as a national right" introduced in July 2017, giving employees, including part-time and casual employees ten-days paid family and domestic violence leave a year (Aeberhard-Hodges & McFerran 2017; McFerron 2011). Within a relatively short period of time, the Australian trade union movement, led by strong leadership from the trade union centre ACTU reached a consensus position. The 2012 ACTU congress policy urged affiliates to include a domestic violence clause in their collective bargaining claims; this was followed by a goal set at the 2015 ACTU congress, for 20-days paid leave for workers experiencing domestic violence to be included in collective bargaining claims. By March 2016, there were 1,234 current union agreements with a domestic violence clause covering over 1 million workers, in a wide range of sectors. Some of the largest employers have agreements covering all workers, as is the case of the 2014 enterprise agreement with the National Australia Bank which gives unlimited paid domestic violence leave if a worker requires it.

The National Tertiary Education Union (NTEU) in Australia has been one of the champions of negotiating progressive clauses in collective agreements. By 2017, about two-thirds of university enterprise agreements included clauses on domestic violence. For example, all universities in the state of Victoria have domestic violence leave for permanent and on-going staff. In 2015, this provision was also extended to casual employees. The union is campaigning for other universities to follow suit. The NTEU model claim for negotiation includes: a) a statement of principle about domestic violence and joint development of policies to address circumstances where an employee is dealing with domestic violence, including referral arrangements to relevant organizations; b) provision that no employee will be disadvantaged in her/his employment because of the consequences of his/her dealing with domestic violence; and c) provision for sufficient special leave for an employee dealing with domestic violence, including seeking safe housing; for medical/counselling appointments; court hearings and legal advice; organizing alternative care or education arrangements for children; and rebuilding support networks with children, family or others (ILO 2018)

ACTU also campaigned for domestic violence leave to be included in the Fair Work Act on the basis that legislation would substantially strengthen collective bargaining with employers by setting a minimum benchmark. The development of alliances and campaigning between unions, experts and the women's movement, the availability of a "model clause" and the commitment of the union representatives are amongst other critical facilitators for these bargaining successes (Baird, McFerran & Wright 2014). Australia also has a relatively strong industrial relations system and unions point to good cooperation with employers on this issue (Gendered Violence Research Network 2015). A critical issue was that some landmark cases were taken through the courts, including a 2015 case on domestic violence and work (*Ms L. Moghimi v. Eliana Construction and Developing Group Pty.Ltd. [2015] FWC 4864, 23/08/2015*), which resulted in the Australian Fair Work Commission ordering an employer to pay maximum compensation for unfair dismissal of a woman worker, who had not been protected from her partner who worked for the same company. In this way, the obligation on employers to provide an "added duty" of care for domestic violence victims in the workplace was firmly established.

Unions in *Canada* have also achieved significant bargaining gains through advocacy and campaigning together with women's organizations and gender experts (MaGregor, Wathen & MacQuarrie 2016). Gender experts have trained workplace representatives and unions on how to implement domestic violence at work programmes and agreements. The CLC's collective bargaining strategy provides seven principles for negotiators to adopt and model language for collective agreements.

In 2017 ITUC launched a global campaign "Stop Gender-Based Violence at Work" for a strong ILO standard on violence and harassment against women and men in the world of work in the form of a convention (and accompanying recommendation). The campaign gained significant traction and visibility globally. Advocacy and awareness-raising campaigns were carried out by women in hundreds of national unions and GUFs across the world. The campaign has also been supported by NGOs and women's organizations across the world. It has been particularly important in persuading workers' organizations, as well as a some governments and employers to back a strong international labour standard that would provide an agreed international definition of violence, including on gender-based violence, and a framework within which governments, employers, companies and unions can take action to tackle the problem and to be held to account for their actions. The campaign has developed resources including a social media campaign, a campaign toolkit (ITUC 2016), a regular newsletter and network. Central to the campaign is the importance of freedom of association and collective bargaining, backed up by a strong enabling legal environment for social dialogue in preventing and tackling violence in the world of work (ITUC undated).

CONCLUSION

This chapter has explored the different innovative ways in which over the last few decades unions have promoted greater gender equality at the workplace through collective agreements, with a particular focus on closing the gender pay gap, maternity and parental leave and working time, and gender-based violence. While many of these issues have the potential to transform gender relations at work, there are a number of barriers to the effectiveness of collective bargaining as a vehicle for change.

The coverage of collective bargaining is primarily in formal employment, and therefore excludes a high proportion of women workers in precarious and informal work. Furthermore, globalization and neoliberalism have led to new forms of work organization and an increase in precarious work through global supply chains, which pose major challenges for unions in organizing and protecting women workers, and particularly young workers, from discrimination. To compound this situation, as mentioned previously, following the economic crisis, there has been a general weakening of collective bargaining even in industrialized countries, as a result of labour market reforms designed to shift collective bargaining from sectoral to company level, and to introduce an increasingly individualized approach. In many countries, austerity measures have often included the freezing of collective bargaining or no cost outcomes. This trend has negative consequences for women's equality generally, and while in some countries, the gender pay gap may have decreased, this is because of the overall degradation of working conditions in male-dominated industries.

Nonetheless, the collective bargaining initiatives explored here offer a truly remarkable picture and sound evidence of the positive transformations towards more gender-just and inclusive work environments as a result of negotiations and CBAs. Many of these initiatives have been championed by women union leaders, or gender or equality groups within trade unions, and are a direct consequence of their sustained advocacy. In the food, hotel, catering and agricultural sectors, the IUF adopted a landmark resolution on "menstruation – a workplace and trade union issue". The resolution adopted at the 2017 congress, where the first women general gecretary at the IUF was elected, calls upon "IUF and its affiliates to work to raise awareness about issues around menstruation and ensure that there is access to toilets and sanitary facilities in all workplaces. IUF affiliates shall work actively to prevent and counteract exclusion from education, work or society due to menstruation" (IUF 2017).

Although in some contexts, inevitably, there are still barriers for women to access crucial leadership positions and take part in negotiating teams, and a lack of awareness from male colleagues about the need to adopt gender-sensitive approaches in negotiations and agreements, these limitations should not detract from the overall trend whereby trade unions have transformed into the twenty-first century champions of social justice, gender equality, inclusion and diversity. As part of this transformation, the linkages and coordination with other civil society organizations, in particular women's groups and development NGOs, has been strengthened and consolidated.

Gender pay gap

Trade unions recognize the multifaceted structural issues of tackling the gender pay gap, including working time, occupational segregation, the unequal sharing of domestic work, child and elder care. In recent years, trade unions, particularly in the public sector, have given priority to initiatives designed to address the persistent gender pay gap. This work has included advocacy on pay transparency at legislative level and negotiations to include pay transparency or pay audits in collective agreements, as the basis on which evidence of pay discrimination can be built.

Unions representing workers in countries with a high gender pay gap have generally placed more emphasis on the structural causes of pay inequalities, such as the undervaluing of women's work, and occupational segregation. Another strategy is to award above average pay rises to workers in female-dominated sectors or agree on special equality allowances. In contrast, unions representing workers in countries with a lower gender pay gap (principally countries in eastern and central Europe) have different negotiating strategies, often primarily focused on low pay and increasing minimum wages across the whole economy. Good practices, for example, on preparation of disaggregated data prior to bargaining, as exists in Sweden and Norway, would be extremely useful in other national contexts, both in Europe and elsewhere. Unions have also successfully negotiated the introduction of new pay and grading schemes with revised job classification methodologies, which seek to remove any gender bias. This approach has been successful not only in many European and North American contexts but is gaining currency in some Latin American countries as well.

Maternity and parental leave

In countries where there is still employer liability for maternity leave allowances, unions have been advocates for the introduction of social insurance schemes and the need to ensure that these schemes cover informal workers as well. In countries with national insurance coverage, and where there are longer leave entitlements, bargaining has also sought to ensure that women on maternity leave do not lose out in terms of career development and/or have entitlements that are extended beyond what is set out in the law. In Europe and many OECD countries, parental and paternity leave is well established in legislation and many collective agreements have extended legal entitlements. In Latin America, paternity leave is increasingly common and is incorporated into many union bargaining agendas. In this context, collective bargaining has been an essential tool at national, sectoral and enterprise level to affirm existing legislative provisions and thus contribute to strengthening compliance and to improve upon legal minimum requirements.

Work–life balance and working time

Most unions in industrialized countries are actively involved in advocacy and bargaining around work–life balance and working time. Innovative agreements regulate working hours, flexibility in working time, rights of part-time workers and rights for workers with parental responsibilities to increase or decrease their working time and leave arrangements for parents, including additional rights for fathers to enable them to participate in family life. Unions have also actively engaged on the issue of predictability of working hours, particularly as the practice of zero working hours' contracts has spread in the "gig economy", often in female-dominated sectors, such as catering.

Gender-based violence and harassment at the workplace, including domestic violence

Women unionists have been longstanding advocates of ensuring that unions have both internal safeguarding policies and that either through additional clauses in collective agreements or stand-alone policies, there are clear procedures to tackle sexual harassment at the workplace. Unions have also carried out training programmes to ensure that union officials understand how to handle grievance procedures related to sexual harassment. Violence and harassment at work is increasingly approached as a core safety and health or well-being at work issue, taking into account the psychosocial risks faced by all workers, and including third party violence and harassment, against workers in client, teaching or patient-facing posts. Campaigning over many years by women unionists and domestic violence organizations has led to recognition in many unions that domestic violence impacts on the workplace and that employers have a "duty of care" to ensure that victims are supported and protected.

The examples in this chapter illustrate how key gender concerns have been successfully mainstreamed into union bargaining priorities. In Australia, for example, McFerron (2016) was able to access the employment workplace agreement database containing a detailed description of the content of existing agreements, which is a resource not available in most countries. Having similar national databases would considerable help unions in tracking clauses in workplace and sectoral agreements. Some of these developments have been integrally linked to trade union renewal, particularly focused on organizing strategies and representing new groups of workers. As Hansen (2004) argues union renewal is closely linked to the integration of diversity and gender equality issues in trade union practices.

In the context of globalization and increasing social inequalities, unions have also worked at the tripartite international level to re-examine the scope of the employment relationship and to address the social protection needs of precarious and informal work outside the reach of traditional collective bargaining. The great majority of employment today is still in small or family enterprises and the overwhelming majority of women work in temporary or precarious jobs, home-based work or the informal economy where trade unions and collective agreements are unlikely to be present. In these situations, other forms of collective organization and bargaining have been taking shape, which are explored further in the next chapter.

4

Changing employment patterns, precarious and informal work, and the challenge for collective bargaining

Over the last decade, following the 2008 global economic crisis, profound changes have taken place in the world of work, particularly affecting women (Bettio *et al.* 2013). Driven by neoliberal policies and global competition and inequalities, along with technological innovations and shifting patterns of production, there has been a concurrent increase in women's employment and migration for work, this latter also fuelled in some measure by wars and climate change (Eaton, Schurman & Chen 2017). These changes have major implications for labour regulations, industrial relations and traditional patterns of collective bargaining (ILO 2017a). This section examines these issues in relation to overall patterns of employment and the extent of precarious and informal work, which particularly affects women, in both developed and developing countries.

THE EXTENT OF PREDOMINANTLY FEMALE PRECARIOUS AND INFORMAL WORK

Precarious work (ITUC 2011a, 2017) or non-standard work in the ILO terminology (ILO 2016b) is found in both developing and developed economies. Of countries with available data, three-quarters of the global workforce are employed on temporary or short-term contracts, in informal jobs often without any contract, under own-account arrangements or in unpaid family jobs (ILO 2015b). Over 60 per cent of all workers lack

Table 4.1: Informal work by region

Region	Informal work (%)
Africa	85.8
Asia Pacific	68.2
Americas	40.0
Europe and Central Asia	25.1

Source: ILO 2018d.

any kind of employment contract. Two billion – or 61.2 per cent – of the world's employed population aged 15 and over work informally, which includes own-account or contributing family work. Informal economy workers can be employers, employees, own-account workers, contributing family workers and members of informal cooperatives. Emerging and developing countries represent 93 per cent of the world's informal employment (ILO 2018d). Table 4.1 shows the proportion of informal employment across different regions. Although increasingly common in industrialized countries, the majority of informal work is found in emerging or developing economies. In Sub-Saharan Africa, more than 90 per cent of the female workforce and 82 per cent of the male workforce are employed in informal work (ILO 2018d).

The growth of precarious work globally has major implications for trade union organizing and recruitment strategies, and for the future of existing models of collective bargaining. In an increasingly fragmented labour market, trade unions and strong labour laws have become yet more important. Although some progress was achieved in reducing precarious work up to 2012, since then, there has been little or no progress. According to the ILO (2018d) the number of workers in precarious forms of employment is predicted to increase by an additional 17 million per year in 2018 and 2019. As the ILO argues:

> Workers in vulnerable forms of employment are typically subject to high levels of precariousness, in that they are more likely to be informally employed, have fewer chances

to engage in social dialogue and are less likely to benefit from job security, regular incomes and access to social protection than their wage and salaried counterparts (ILO 2018d: 6).

In Europe, the informal economy or undeclared work is estimated to amount to 18.4 per cent of the EU's GDP in 2012 (Eurofound 2013b). In sectors such as hospitality, care and domestic work, industrial cleaning and agriculture, there are high levels of young, female and often migrant workers whose situation is often compounded by their undocumented status. Informal and unregulated work is most prevalent in transitional economies of the EU and in countries facing austerity programmes such as Greece, Spain and Portugal. The European Commission's initiative, "Tackling Undeclared Work" launched in May 2016, which brings together the social partners is an indication of the increased recognition and importance given to the issue. Its two-year work programme 2017–18 is designed to build capacity and is limited to sharing transferable practices.

REDEFINING INFORMAL WORK AND EXTENDING THE RECOGNITION OF RIGHTS

In 2002, an ILO conference resolution "Decent work and the informal economy" endorsed a new broad definition of informal employment that includes both self-employed workers in informal enterprises (defined as small unregistered enterprises) and dependent workers in informal jobs (defined as those without protection). This new broader definition has served as a unified framework that includes not only unprotected informal workers in the global south but also unprotected non-standard workers in the global north.

The ILO 2015 Recommendation 204 on the "Transition from the informal to the formal economy" gives recognition to workers in the informal economy and is designed to assist workers claim their rights and strengthen access to social protection. This landmark ILO Recommendation also recognizes that informal employment is predominantly female. It acknowledges that women experience discrimination and segregation in the labour market not only on the basis of their gender, but also on the basis of their class, race, ethnicity, age, sexual orientation, sexual identity, disability, HIV status and migration status. Persistent gender-based violence is often used to prevent women from asserting individual and collective rights. It followed the adoption of the ILO 2012 Recommendation 202 on National Social Protection Floors which recognized the primary responsibility of the state to provide basic social security guarantees, the universality of protection, based on social solidarity and social inclusion, so that workers in the informal economy are also covered.

The great majority of the female workforce is concentrated in sectors characterized by contract, casual or family labour, precarious employment and informality, for example, in agricultural work, home-based work, street vending and domestic work. This work is predominantly low-paid and disproportionately female (ILO 2014b; Bonner, StreetNet International & WIEGO 2009; Chant & Pedwell 2008). This is an issue relevant to both developing and developed economies. As Eaton, Chen and Schurman (2017: 1) argue, "informal workers, their organizations and their campaigns, represent the leading edge of the most significant change in the global labor movement in more than a century".

UNION INITIATIVES TO EXTEND COLLECTIVE BARGAINING TO WORKERS IN INFORMAL AND PRECARIOUS WORK

Women's organizing and the extension of collective bargaining to workers in precarious and informal work represents a significant new development, showing the widening reach of trade unions and collaboration between unions and informal workers' organizations. Women's agency has led to more proactive union strategies in organizing and advocating for women workers in exploited, isolated and precarious working situations, including migrant and ethnic minority workers, child and bonded labour and situations of modern-day slavery, or those at risk of trafficking (ILO 2013b; Pillinger 2017b). In recent decades, there has been a convergence of initiatives from trade unions and the women's movement, coordinated most prominently by the global network of Women in Informal Employment Globalizing and Organizing (WIEGO), with the result that the collective voice of women informal workers has been considerably strengthened.

From the trade union perspective, in the developed world, unions are confronting the erosion of formal employment as a consequence of outsourcing, temporary and contract work, and new forms of dependent self-employment or triangular relations whereby the main contractor seeks to evade responsibility for the employment conditions of the workforce. At the same time, and as a consequence of both globalization and the increasing prominence of women in trade unions and their growing influence on the union agenda, in developing countries unions have identified new organizing priorities to address workers' rights in the subcontracting supply chain, often migrant or seasonal workers, such as women garment workers, or in horticulture or home-based workers. As the ITUC argues, it is women's organizing initiatives that led to negotiations for bargaining rights to protect women workers in previously unprotected sectors, with a transformational role in rethinking the unions' organizing priorities. As Chidi King, ITUC's equality director states:

> Women are driving new forms of organizing and recruitment, for example, of informal workers, domestic workers and women working at the bottom of global supply chains in the horticulture and garments sectors. Women have also set new trade union agendas specifically in areas such as maternity protection, social protection, childcare and violence against women.[1]

Many national trade union centres have revised their constitutions so that informal economy workers and their associations can become members and have developed strategies to extend appropriate services to these workers. While there are on-going discussions concerning

---

1. Interview with Chidi King, Brussels, 21 January 2016 with the authors.

different organizing models, at present, there is a flexible or dual approach whereby some membership-based organizations have developed into registered trade unions at national level, or indeed have been established by the unions, as their informal economy "wing" or special group, while others have remained associations or networks. This flexibility allows sufficient space to tap into the impetus of innovative organizing methods and building transnational networks and coalitions, while in turn the unions or associations of informal workers can benefit from elements of formal organizational structures, negotiating skills and added legitimacy (ILO 2013b).

More recently, commitments to organize workers in the informal economy have merged with initiatives to address the increasing incidence of precarious and own-account work in sectors where employment was previously more stable and enjoyed some minimum social security coverage. For example, the Trade Union Confederation of the Americas (TUCA) adopted a trade union strategy on precarious and informal workers at its third congress in 2016, which ratified its commitment to promote the extension of rights to informal economy workers, with particular attention to women, young persons, Afro-descendants and migrant workers. The resolution also ratified the Confederation's commitment to promote informal economy organizations, legislative initiatives and support for collective bargaining with a gender perspective (TUCA 2016).

As labour markets have become increasingly fragmented, trade unions in Europe and other OECD countries have also given attention to organizing and negotiating CBAs for low-paid workers, part-time workers, casual workers and care workers, many of whom in the past were outside the scope of collective agreements (Pillinger 2014). The five main areas which have been addressed are (1) setting limits to the time and extent of contract work; (2) agreements to reduce or eliminate wage differentials between regular and contract workers; (3) guarantees for a minimum number of working hours; (4) the extension of maternity protection and (5) occupational health and safety provisions (Pillinger 2014). Some of these initiatives have been extended to home workers, an example of which is South Australia's Fair Work Act, which was amended in 2012 to regulate the entire supply chain in the textile, footwear, and clothing industries and to include homeworkers. However, the implementation and enforcement of legislation to protect homeworkers is limited, even where countries have ratified ILO Convention 177 on home-based workers. An increasing number of trade union and NGO initiatives have extended their reach to include home-based workers.

One example is the Occupational Safety, Health and Environment Foundation (OSHE) in Bangladesh, which is a specialized labour foundation that includes homeworkers in the textile sector in its remit, and protects the safety of homeworkers. One area of work includes economic violence (such us withholding of pay) by employers and labour brokers, as well as ensuring that women receive their pay rather than it going directly to their husbands.[2]

TRADE UNIONS IN AFRICA ADOPT COMMITMENTS TO ORGANIZE INFORMAL WORKERS

In *Ghana*, the Trade Union Congress (GTUC) established a policy whereby it encouraged its sector-based member unions to include informal economy workers. Unions were also encouraged to review their constitution and structures so that they could mainstream informal economy members into their activities, whether as part of their unions directly or as independent affiliates.

The Ugandan Amalgamated Transport and General Workers Union (UATGWU) established the Informal Sector Women's Committee, with the support of the ITF, and organized informal women transport workers and women working in and around major transport hubs, leading to negotiations to improve women's safety and access to toilet and other facilities and greater visibility of the problems faced by informal women workers (ITF 2016; Pillinger 2017b). This has resulted in an increase in the union's membership, largely through the affiliation of associations of informal transport workers, organizing and support to GALIMA (an all-women association of survivors of HIV and AIDS in transport) and traders and home-based workers organized through the Tukolere Wamu Craft Development Association. The establishment of the UATGWU Informal Sector Women's Committee and local women's committees have helped to raise women's awareness of their rights and reporting on violations of rights and abuse (ITF 2017).

---

2. Information provided by Saki Rezwana, chair of OSHE, Bangladesh.

Trade unions in OECD countries develop strategies to organize precarious workers

In *Austria*, a collective agreement for temporary workers was established in 2002, one of the first in Europe. In 2013, PRO-GE that organizes in the food and agricultural industries surveyed 230 large companies and found that 53 per cent of so-called "temporary" workers were working continuously throughout the year. From 2013, a new law was introduced so that temporary workers must receive equal treatment, in particular social benefits, with regular workers. In *Belgium*, a system of "service cheques" has been introduced whereby companies that register receive tax benefits and workers are given legal contracts and can register in the social security system. The CSC trade union centre is supporting domestic and care workers to enable them to benefit from the new regulations. In *Switzerland*, a system of "service cheques" also exists, whereby employers in private households can register domestic workers in the social security system even though they are working on an hourly system.[3]

In *Australia*, unions have also focused on organizing women care workers, who often work in small, dispersed workplaces and have traditionally been poorly organized (Bailey *et al.* 2014). In Queensland, Australia, following a pay equity campaign "Good Work – Decent Wages" by the Queensland Services Union and the Queensland Council of Social Service, a historic decision on pay equity was made by the Queensland Industrial Relations Commission in 2009. The decision benefitted more than 20,000 low-paid social and community services sector workers (Rhee & Zabin 2009; Parker *et al.* 2011).

Education unions across the world have given priority to organizing and negotiating for workers in early childhood education, where many workers work informally and have not previously been members of trade unions nor covered by agreements. In many countries, there is insufficient distinction between informal childcare work and professional provision of early childhood education because of workers' relatively low status and earnings and widespread use of informal contracts. Initiatives to set global standards, through an ILO global dialogue forum, have emphasized the importance of social dialogue in order to regulate the sector, set minimum professional and employment standards, and

---

3. See https://www.chequeservice.ch/fr/questions-frequentes (accessed 24 September 2018).

promote union membership and collective bargaining coverage. In this way, informal work is being transformed into formal employment and greater visibility and value given to a predominantly female workforce. For example, teachers' unions in the USA have developed innovative strategies, engaging both parents and workers, carrying out organizing and advocacy for funding, minimum standards and laws to enforce the quality of early childhood education (EI 2012).

Considerable effort has been given to developing collective agreements for workers in early childhood education, of whom 90 per cent are women. In some countries, this sector is unregulated and in others, it is regulated by the public sector but carried out by private actors.[4]

MEMBERSHIP-BASED ORGANIZATIONS OF INFORMAL WORKERS IN WOMEN-DOMINATED SECTORS AND ALLIANCES WITH TRADE UNIONS

New union initiatives to organize informal workers have coincided with the growth of grassroots informal economy membership-based organizations, many in women-dominated sectors, such as domestic work, street-vending, waste-picking and home-based workers. Their formation was a response to both the growth of women's informal employment as well as the lack of capacity of unions to organize workers in the informal sector. The Self-Employed Women's Association (SEWA) established in 1972 in India (Kapoor 2007) and expanded with the foundation of WIEGO in 1998 was one of the pioneer organizations.

THE DEVELOPMENT OF SEWA AND WIEGO

The Self-Employed Women's Association (SEWA) has a dual cooperative and trade union structure. SEWA provides a range of services to members, including savings and credit, health and childcare, insurance, legal aid and capacity

---

4. Interview with Haldis Holst, EI deputy general secretary, Brussels, 21 January 2016 with the authors.

building, to enable women to become self-reliant. SEWA also supports members in negotiations with employers to improve working conditions.

SEWA was formed in 1972, initially as part of a larger trade union, the Textile Labour Association (TLA) of mill workers in Ahmedabad, an affiliate of the then International Federation of Textile, Garment and Leather Workers Federation (ITGWLF). It lost its membership of the TLA over its position in favour of lower castes. It was finally recognized in its own right as a national federation when it reached 500,000 members in 2005. It is affiliated at international level to the two global unions IUF and IndustriAll. In 2006, it became an affiliate to the ICFTU (now ITUC). When SEWA applied for affiliation to the ITUC, it was challenged to prove in what way it engaged in collective bargaining. In response, SEWA reported it had identified 102 collective agreements with bidi cigarette manufacturers, incense manufactures, tobacco-processing, municipal corporations, fruit cooperatives and others to which its member organizations were signatories (SEWA 2006). This marked in many ways the culmination of a rapprochement between the formal trade union movement and the women workers' cooperatives and networks.

In 2016, SEWA's membership amounted to over 1,300,000 self-employed women, from street-vending, home-based workers, such as garment and bidi cigarette makers, manual labourers in agriculture and construction, and producers, such as small-scale farmers. SEWA has many organizing achievements. For example, in March 2016, SEWA won a major victory for informal sector workers in the state of Gujarat (India) in the form of government issued identity cards. The identity cards grant recognition as workers and entitlement to access to free health and accident insurance for workers and their families. Tens of thousands of workers have already received their identity cards, including street food vendors, vegetable sellers, cooks' helpers and food servers as well as agricultural and rural workers (IUF 2016).

Women in Informal Employment Globalizing and Organizing (WIEGO), founded in 1998, is a global network focused on securing livelihoods for the working poor, especially women, in the informal economy. SEWA was one of its founding members. WIEGO carries out research, statistical analysis and facilitates organization and network building, through capacity building and exchanges. WIEGO also helps informal workers' organizations with fund-raising, through information, practical support and collaborative projects.

Since 2000, and with the support of WIEGO, several transnational networks of organizations of predominantly female informal workers have been formed or consolidated. They include StreetNet International (2002), HomeNet South Asia (2000), Latin American Waste Pickers Network (Red Lacre) (2005), International Domestic Workers' Network (IDWN) (2009), the

Global Alliance of Waste Pickers (2009), HomeNet Eastern Europe (2013), and the International Domestic Workers Federation (IDWF) (2013). These organizations in the main have a female leadership and, for example, Streetnet International provides for gender parity in its decision-making structures and senior leadership.

Over the last two decades, the relations between formal trade unions and organizations of informal workers have strengthened considerably. Particularly in developing country contexts where the vast majority of the workforce is employed in the informal economy, trade unions have undertaken a range of organizing initiatives. However, although these alliances remain uneven across labour categories and countries (Wintour/StreetNet International 2014; ILO/WIEGO 2017), there were, and are, many examples of successful collaboration.

The support of trade unions can significantly increase the negotiating power of the informal workers' associations or cooperatives. SEWA recognizes the benefits of a mutually supportive dual union–cooperative organizational structure. Other examples include Kamala Karki, in Nepal, an organization of home-based garment workers that receives support from the Trade Union Congress in Nepal. In Brazil, a number of waste pickers' cooperatives receive assistance from the Metal Workers' Union, and in some cities, such as Rio de Janeiro, Salvador, São Paulo and Manaus, the CUT trade union has affiliated and supported street-vendors organizations (Wintour 2012). In Argentina, the trade union centres have established and affiliated street vendors' organizations and waste pickers' organizations or general informal economy workers alliances (ILO/WIEGO 2017).

Many of the alliances created between informal women's associations and unions have been developed and consolidated at international level as a result of joint advocacy campaigns, such as the campaign for the ILO Recommendation 204 concerning the transition from the informal to the formal economy. However, some activists initially found this process an uphill climb: "Transnational networks of informal workers, beginning with home-based workers, have struggled to break through the structural constraints and resistance of trade unions to find an equal and respected voice in the ILO" (Bonner, Horn & Jhabvala 2018). By

2009, when the campaign for the adoption of the ILO Convention 189 on domestic workers was launched, there was a strong functioning alliance between trade unions, membership-based organizations and women's organizations. The IUF provided a base for the domestic workers' network to develop as a semi-autonomous body within the organization, and thus providing recognition and legitimacy and contacts within the union movement at different levels. More recently, the proposal for a new ILO standard on violence and harassment against women and men in the world of work has wide-ranging support from both trade unions and informal workers' alliances across the world (see Chapter 3).

RECOGNITION AND BARGAINING IN THE CONTEXT OF THE INFORMAL ECONOMY: GAINS FOR WOMEN

For informal economy workers, priority areas for negotiation are first and foremost recognition as workers, bringing access to legal protection and therefore protection from abuse from authorities, access to health services and pension schemes, and improvements to working conditions and incomes. Other issues include addressing gender inequalities and gender-based violence, housing, childcare and provision of storage or work space, provision of basic sanitation services, minimum piece rates or minimum wages, access to credit and training. Negotiating partners include contractors or individuals working for contractors, local councils and national governments. Social gains, particularly around access to non-contributory social security schemes, have been a result of a combination of factors, including the increased bargaining and representation by informal economy associations, and the adoption of pro-poor policies by governments seeking to address socio-economic inequalities. Examples include Brazil, Colombia and Argentina, this latter with the introduction of the simplified tax and insurance scheme, known as the *Monotributo*, designed for own-account workers (Wintour 2012).

However, in informal economy contexts, negotiations still tend to be around ad hoc issues although there is increasing focus on trying to formalize negotiating or dialogue forums and reach agreements on their mandate and composition. Even in contexts where bargaining forums appear well established, unless there is a statutory commitment to negotiate, agreements are too dependent on the vagaries of political will.[5]

In order to ensure that women's voice and concerns are heard, particularly in work environments where women face discrimination and violence, a number of strategies have been adopted by unions and women's organizations. These include establishing representative participation of women in leadership or coordination positions and creating specific gender-focused training programmes, on issues ranging from literacy, management and public speaking, and issues of sexuality and women's health. Another strategy has been to set up gender forums or committees within the informal economy organizations.

Home-based workers

Home-based work accounts for a significant share of urban employment in some countries: 18 per cent in India, 6 per cent in South Africa. The ILO Convention on Home Work, 1996 (No. 177), however, has only been ratified by ten countries. While Argentina and Thailand have passed legislation specific to home-based workers, other countries, including Brazil, Hong Kong, Peru and South Africa, have not ratified the convention but have incorporated home-based workers into legislation regulating labour relations. Home-based workers have also been included through supply chain legislation.

Home-based workers negotiate with governments, enterprises or middlemen working on their behalf, and with international and local buyers. However, in many cases, the employment relationship is not clear, and the home-based workers negotiate through bargaining with the immediate employer or contractor on issues such as the piece rate, and do not enter negotiations more broadly concerning working conditions and benefits. Home-based workers also negotiate with national

---

5. Interview by Nora Wintour with Chris Bonner, WIEGO organizing and representation emeritus advisor, 9 March 2018.

governments on issues such as the application of existing laws, inclusion in the social security system and access to training and resources (ILO/WIEGO 2017).

In February 2015, 60 networks, associations and trade unions of home-based workers, together with NGOs and researchers met in New Delhi at the Global Conference of Home-based Workers, jointly organized by HomeNet South Asia (HNSA) and WIEGO. They adopted a declaration outlining their main demands, including recognition as workers, whether self-employed or contract workers, and the right to freedom of association and collective bargaining. The declaration stated: "Homeworkers must enjoy the right to collective bargaining and formal collective agreements with lead firms, suppliers and contractors, and with governments (including with local government)" (WIEGO 2015).

Home-based workers also advocate for the extension and enforcement of labour laws and protection and implementation of other supportive laws and regulations appropriate for both the self-employed home-based workers and the subcontracted homeworkers. These main demands were presented to the ASEAN member states in October 2017 in Manila and include: the right to fair prices in markets and fair piece-rates; the right to secure contracts and work orders and commercial transactions; protection from being subjected to poor quality raw materials, arbitrary cancellation of work orders, arbitrary rejection of goods, or delayed payments; the right to labour inspection and complaint resolution mechanisms; and the promotion of formal collective agreements with employers and/or with governments (as per ILO Convention 98).

GOOD PRACTICE EXAMPLES OF COLLECTIVE BARGAINING FOR HOME-BASED WORKERS

The organization of *Thai* home-based workers by HomeNet, Thailand with support from WIEGO, resulted in collective bargaining for the extension of universal health coverage to informal workers and the passing of the Homeworkers Protection Act, which grants Thai home-based workers protection from occupational health and safety risks, minimum wages and other fundamental labour rights enacted in May 2011 (UNDP 2015). This followed a decade of campaigning by HomeNet Thailand and WIEGO. The law established the responsibility of the employer towards the home-based workers by requiring the contractor to provide a work contract. It includes measures to ensure regular payment of fair wages, equal pay for men and women, and the employer's responsibility to ensure occupational health and safety. The law establishes a home-based workers' committee that provides access to the courts in labour disputes. HomeNet Thailand has helped groups register to get the right to vote for representatives on the committee. Amendments to the Social Security Act (article 40) establish a voluntary scheme whereby the government will pay between 30–50 per cent of the worker's contributions to a social security fund to entitle informal workers to sickness, disability, survivor's and old-age benefits. In 2012, the government adopted an Action Plan 2012–16, involving nine ministries, to enhance the capacity of the government administration to engage with informal workers and which envisages establishing a first national committee on informal workers. HomeNet Thailand considers the new social security scheme could assist as many as 24 million informal workers, the majority of whom are women.

Domestic workers

The adoption of the ILO Domestic Workers Convention, 2011 (No. 189) and its accompanying Recommendation (No. 201) was a major landmark in extending organizing and bargaining rights for a largely unprotected female-dominated sector. Despite a growth in domestic workers' organizations, collective bargaining to improve basic rights, minimum wages and decent working conditions for domestic workers remains limited. In the majority of countries, there is no minimum wage setting for domestic workers. An ILO study (Oelz & Rani 2015) of selected developing countries found no CBAs in the domestic work sector, although in a rapidly increasing number of countries trade unions have been formed to protect the rights of domestic workers, which is the first essential step towards negotiating a collective agreement. The International Domestic Workers Federation (IDWF) was founded in 2013 and regional networks and national unions in many countries are playing a key role in promoting decent work and compliance with the ILO Convention 189 (Oelz & Rani 2015). In 2017, the IDWF had grown to include 62 affiliates in 50 countries and was affiliated to the global union, IUF, as a special group. The IDWF has developed a specific focus on organizing migrant and refugee domestic workers in the context of the care economy, on safe migration and on the issue of sexual harassment and its impact on domestic workers. In order for collective bargaining to take place, formal legislation is not sufficient. Blackett (2017) argues that capacity building for domestic workers, combined with implementation incentives for employers and robust enforcement by governments is also required.

In some OECD countries, new legislation has regulated basic working conditions. In the USA for example, legislation to protect the basic labour rights of domestic workers has now been adopted in eight states. In Nevada, for example, the new law, known as the Domestic Workers' Bill of Rights, came into effect in 2018 and regulates mandatory minimum payment, working hours, overtime, rest breaks and holiday entitlements and limits any deductions that can be made for the provision of food or lodging. In other states, unions have been able to negotiate innovative agreements to benefit domestic workers. In California, boards have been formed that include representatives from government, placement agencies, the domestic workers' union, and of organizations representing the clients (elderly, disabled or otherwise in need of home care) to negotiate basic working conditions (ILO 2015a).

Some unions, for example in Belgium, Austria, Sweden and Italy, have negotiated agreements to protect the rights of domestic workers (Pillinger 2014). In Belgium, an agreement between the social partners led to a commitment to negotiate on wages and working conditions of domestic workers. In Italy, the first collective agreement on domestic workers dates back to 1974 and has been revised every four years, covering broad range of issues related to pay and conditions of employment of domestic workers. The Swiss confederation SGB/USS, negotiated a national "standard work contract", setting out minimum wages and working conditions for domestic workers. In 2012 the Spanish confederation, CCOO negotiated improvements in the minimum pay and negotiations on the new regulation for domestic workers after their recent incorporation to the general social security system, resulting in major improvements in the working conditions and social protection rights of domestic workers.

GOOD PRACTICE EXAMPLES OF ORGANIZING AND
BARGAINING FOR DOMESTIC WORKERS

Uruguay was the first country to ratify ILO Convention 189 and is among the countries with the most advanced legislation in terms of protecting domestic workers. With the support of the gender department of the PIT-CNT trade union centre, domestic workers created the first national union representing domestic workers (Goldsmith 2013). Collective bargaining on employment conditions in domestic work was established in 2006, when the law regulating the domestic work sector was adopted. The collective agreement, covering the period from January 2013 to December 2015, benefits more than 120,000 domestic workers. It was negotiated in a tripartite commission, with representatives from the Ministry of Labour and Social Security, the Trade Union of Domestic Workers (SUTD), and the employers' association, the Housewives League (*Liga de Amas de Casa*). The agreement raises the domestic workers' minimum wage and sets adjustment rates according to three salary bands, with a salary increase of 37.6 per cent for the lowest band, 26.6 per cent for the middle band and 13.7 per cent for the highest band. The outcome of previous rounds of negotiation in 2008 and 2010 included a premium for time in service, compensation for night work, and the creation of the Domestic Worker Day on August 19 as a paid holiday. The group also agreed to form a tripartite commission on occupational health (Espino & Pedetti 2012).

In *Kenya*, an agreement for hotel and domestic workers initiated by the Kenya Union of Domestic, Hotels, Educational Institutions, Hospitals and Allied Workers (KUDHEIHA), was possible because of legislation introduced in 2008 giving new rights to Kenya's domestic workers. The agreement between KUDHEIHA and the Union of the Kenya Hotelkeepers and Caterers Association was signed on 1 July 2014 for a two-year period and for the first time covers a large number of women working in hotels and in domestic work. It introduced a minimum wage, a general wage increase for all workers of 9 per cent and an additional 9 per cent increase in housing allowances. Female employees have an entitlement to three months maternity leave on full pay and an additional 26 working days of annual leave during the year of maternity leave. Male employees are entitled to 14 days paternity leave in respect of childbirth for legally married partners.

Waste-pickers

Waste pickers have been mobilizing collectively to demand formal incorporation into municipal waste management systems. In so doing, Dias and Samson (2016) argue, waste pickers are transforming relations between the state, the formal economy and the informal economy, and indeed contributing to pathways towards a more inclusive, participatory and democratic state. The waste pickers' associations or cooperatives negotiate with enterprises or contractors and also with governments or local authorities, on issues such as security, access to public spaces and markets, legal recognition and protection, as well as inclusion in public waste management systems (ILO/WIEGO 2017). The support of larger organizations and networks can significantly increase the negotiating power of the waste pickers.

In addition, women waste pickers face multiple forms of violence and initiatives have sought to empower women to raise awareness of the need to include gender demands in the waste pickers' collective claims at the local, state and national level (Dias & Ogando 2015). In Brazil, women's experiences of violence and harassment and their proposals for action were shared through dialogues with men and women leaders in waste pickers' cooperatives and the national waste picker movement to raise awareness on the need for collectively addressing barriers to gender equality (Dias & Ogando 2015).

GOOD PRACTICE EXAMPLE OF ORGANIZING AND BARGAINING FOR WASTE PICKERS

In 2003, *Colombia*'s High Court granted waste pickers the right to work and status as workers, the first ruling of its kind that legally protected waste pickers' services in Latin America. This was a result of the advocacy of the Association for Recyclers of Bogotá (*Asociación de Recicladores de Bogotá*), considered a pioneer in the protection of waste pickers' rights. In 2011, the constitutional court ordered Bogotá's waste management system to include waste pickers in its tendering process. Women lead many of the city's recycling cooperatives and associations. The organization put forward negotiating positions concerning the public policy that the municipality should adopt, including secure and guaranteed access to recyclable materials, security for professional waste pickers to remain in the profession and recognition of a payment system for cleansing and environmental services. These proposals were designed to help establish a path to greater levels of employment formalization.

In Pune, India, waste pickers' organizations campaigned for over 20 years to achieve recognition for their work, assert their status as workers and to become public services providers (Chikarmane 2012). In Brazil, waste pickers have organized at municipal level in some cities and the Federal government set up the inter-ministerial committee for the social inclusion of waste-pickers in August 2006, which met regularly with the National Movement of Waste Pickers (MNCR). This led to the National Policy of Solid Waste adopted in July 2010. In Minas Gerais, the State Solid Waste Policy approved in 2009 recognizes the role of cooperatives in waste management, includes clauses on social inclusion of waste pickers and economic incentives for municipalities to abide by the law. This led to the first recycling bonus law to increase the cooperative workers' income. There are now initiatives to extend social protection, including retirement pensions and maternity protection to waste pickers (Dias & Cardoso Silva 2017). The formal integration of waste pickers into the municipal waste management system in Belo Horizonte, Brazil, fundamentally transformed and democratized both the system itself and the way that the state relates to waste pickers and residents (Dias & Cidrin 2008).

In Argentina, there have been similar initiatives, designed to foster the self-organization of waste pickers, to register their organizations so that members are entitled to a license and protective clothing, as well as access to a variety of training programmes and medical coverage. The Law on Zero Waste (*Basura Cero*) 2006 also calls for the effective participation of urban recyclers in the design of plans, and in inspection and control.

In 2005, the Latin American Waste Pickers' Network, (Red LACRE) was formed, which now has 15 national associations. The First World Conference of Waste Pickers was held in 2008 in Bogota, Colombia with the subsequent formation of the Global Alliance of Waste Pickers. The alliance had 99 network members in January 2018.

Street vendors

The great majority of street vendors operate without licenses and are consequently subjected to police harassment, forced to pay bribes and can face confiscation of their goods, eviction from their trading sites, and on occasion, police brutality, arrest and detention. Street vendors are not a homogenous group. However, most street vendors are poor and low-skilled, and take up trading as the only option available to them, because of the low start-up costs and flexible hours. Traders can work long hours, sometimes more than 12 hours per day, their workplaces are insecure, storage for goods is often a problem, and they are subjected to traffic pollutants and inclement weather, which can take a particular toll on young infants who accompany their mothers. They are generally not registered in state social security systems (Roever & Skinner 2016). Studies suggest that women tend to earn less than their male counterparts, because they have less well-situated trading sites, with poorer installations and security, and they tend to trade in perishable goods, while men sell higher value goods, such as electronics (Chen & Snodgrass 2001).

Because street vendors operate on the margins of the law, the issue of their legal status is a major concern, particularly trading permits or licenses. In most countries, trading is regulated by municipal by-laws and ordinances, which often prohibit trading in public spaces. These by-laws are enforced irregularly, depending on political interests and urban renewal policies. The possibilities for street vendors' organizations to dialogue with the authorities are generally quite limited.

One of the main demands of StreetNet International and its affiliate organizations is to set up bargaining forums with street vendors where the issues and demands of informal traders can be discussed with the relevant authorities (StreetNet International 2012). In India, following a successful campaign by the National Alliance of Street Vendors of India (NASVI), the federal government enacted the Street Vendors (Protection of Livelihood and Regulation of Street Vending) Act, 2014, that mandates state governments to frame a scheme for its implementation by municipal corporations under the direction of town vending committees. This new law allows for the registration and licensing of street vendors, who are often subjected to harassment and demands for illegal payments. It also established rights for compensation or alternative sites in cases of relocation, a permanent committee to review grievances and other disputes, and local authorities are called on to establish street vending plans in consultation with representative organizations (NASVI 2014).

Through municipal tripartite dialogue committees on own-account workers in Central America (Costa Rica, El Salvador, and Honduras), where over 60–70 per cent of employment is informal, the main trade union centres have established federations of informal workers or own-account workers and have supported advocacy for new legislative initiatives, in particular for own-account workers which would provide legal recognition and access to social security. With support from the ILO, municipal tripartite dialogue committees were established to review municipal level regulatory reforms and in some cases, trade unions have worked with market associations to support negotiations over the development of new market infrastructure.[6]

Other informal economy or precarious work

Unions have improved women's representation and decision-making roles in other informal or precarious work settings, through training and awareness-raising on existing legislation and protections, and through developing bargaining strategies in a participative manner.

---

6. ILO project to promote respect for labour rights of informal workers in Costa Rica, El Salvador and Honduras. Available at http://www.ilo.org/sanjose/programas-y-proyectos/WCMS_206470/lang--es/index.htm (accessed 24 September 2018).

EXAMPLES OF UNION ORGANIZING AND BARGAINING
FOR INFORMAL WORKERS

In *India*, with the support of the International Transport Federation, the Maharashra State Transport Kamgar Sanghatana Union (MSTKS) has disseminated information about India's Sexual Harassment Act (2013). In November 2015, an alliance of transport unions, passengers' associations and NGOs launched a campaign to end violence against women in transport. The campaign led to workplace improvements, such as separate toilet facilities for women bus drivers, and unions taking up new issues such as sexual harassment and the high levels of miscarriages faced by women conductors. One of the positive outcomes of the campaign was that more women joined the union, which has since strengthened women's advocacy (ITF 2017).

The All India Brick and Tiles Manufacturers Federation (AIBTMF) and the Building and Wood Workers' International (BWI) signed a formal memorandum of understanding in 2008 on child and forced labour, equal treatment for migrant workers and set up a joint coordination committee to resolve issues of concern. The sector is characterized by the use of the piece-rate wage system, which encourages family labour, including child and bonded labour. Conditions are generally extremely poor and women lack separate toilets or childcare facilities. The adoption of the new federal sexual harassment legislation in 2013 offered an opportunity to address the many problems of harassment and violence faced by women workers. The brick kiln unions affiliated to BWI in Punjab, Bijar and Uttar Pradesh set up women's self-help groups to raise awareness and identify issues and have taken up cases of intimidation and harassment of women workers (BWI 2017).

In *Spain*, the Spanish Union of Professional Autonomous Workers (UPTA), affiliated to the UGT, organizes a wide range of workers, including street vendors. In 2010, Royal Decree 1613/2010 set out the establishment of the Council of Autonomous Work, which provides for the institutional representation of self-employed workers in order to develop supportive public services. Tripartite consultative regional councils exist in Navarra, Andalucía and Extremadura, with a mandate to review socio-economic and professional matters, including measures to reduce occupational and health risks and to extend social security protection, as well as conflict resolution mechanisms. In Andalucía, the strategic plan on autonomous work makes reference to the need to include a gender perspective, reconciliation of work and family based on the principle of coresponsibility and programmes to promote equal opportunities and co-ownership of any business enterprise (art.3(1), art.5(2)g; art. 6(2)). In Madrid, UPTA supports its affiliate organization, the

Association of Autonomous Women Workers and Entrepreneurs in negotiations with the municipality in order to provide training and advice on setting up small businesses (StreetNet International 2012).

CONCLUSION

Over the last two decades, there has been a substantive growth in the number of initiatives to strengthen the organization and representation of women workers in precarious and informal work both in developing and developed countries. Cooperation between informal workers' organizations and trade unions contributes to strengthening bargaining power, agency and voice of women, and offers mutual support. Unions have supported advocacy work on both negotiations with government at national, provincial and local level on issues such as workers' inclusion in social protection schemes, in training programmes on organization and negotiating skills and on occupational safety and health. However, this has not been without its challenges, where employment is informal or precarious, particularly in sectors where it is difficult to identify an appropriate employer or employers' organization, such as a local authority, with which to negotiate.

While some organizations have a specific gender focus, such as women's cooperatives, others are membership-based organizations operating in female-dominated low-paid sectors. Some have also been directly established as trade unions, or some with support from trade union centres or sectoral trade union federations. Registering as a cooperative or association of workers is clearly a first step to achieve recognition, status and bargaining power. Establishing alliances with, or affiliation to, other cooperatives, social movements or trade unions at local, national and regional levels has also been contributing factors to the success in enabling informal economy workers to engage in negotiations with local and national governments, advocate for new laws and monitor their enforcement.

This chapter has argued that building alliances and affiliations is crucial in enabling informal economy workers to engage in negotiations with local and national governments. However, it is equally true that in many cases over the last two decades, key social gains have been as much a consequence of wider political, labour and social reforms achieved as the result of the election of governments committed to inclusive social protection policies.

5

The global dimension of collective bargaining: the role of global framework agreements in promoting gender equality

This chapter examines existing mechanisms for collective bargaining between multinational enterprises (MNEs) and global union federations (GUFs) as effective spaces for gender equality bargaining. It looks at the role and potential of collective bargaining and ways in which gender equality is promoted through regional and global framework agreements covering workers in MNEs including in global supply chains. Global and regional framework agreements between MNEs and GUFs have been used to promote workers' rights and gender equality across global supply chains. In the last decade, there has been a marked trend to strengthen gender equality and diversity clauses in these agreements, particularly in female-dominated employment sectors.

In many countries, however, GUFs and their national affiliates are faced with major challenges concerning workers' rights, including violations of the right to freedom of association and the right to bargain collectively, as documented in the annual Global Rights Index of the International Trade Union Confederation (ITUC 2017). Corporate social responsibility initiatives often fail to respect ILO conventions or address the responsibility of business enterprises for their adverse impacts on human rights in the supply chain and in the local communities (ITUC 2011a). Furthermore, many women work in global production sites in non-unionized export processing zones (EPZs), where contract labour is used to produce goods for global supply chains (ILO 2016a; Morris & Pillinger 2016). As Hadwiger (2015) argues, EPZ workers are typically "female, young, migrant and poor, with no trade union experience and no knowledge of their rights" (14).

WOMEN'S WORK IN GLOBAL PRODUCTION

Women's employment in MNEs is often of a better quality than in domestic enterprises, and waged work in export factories in the garment sector is an alternative to working in the informal economy (OECD 2008). When women have access to employment, household poverty is reduced and family members have better access to resources that benefit the education and health of other household members (DFID/IDRC 2012; UN Women 2015). However, many women working in global production sites face significant problems of exploitation, low pay, poor working conditions, lack of social protection, long working hours and low union representation. Furthermore, some of the fastest growing developing countries show the least signs of progress on gender equality. As a result, it is evident that: "formal regular waged work has the greatest transformative potential for women, but this potential has remained limited because of the lack of creation of decent jobs, and because of segmentation of labour markets" (DFID/IDRC 2012: 3). Women are concentrated in the most exploited segments of global supply chains, subjected to the demands of MNEs for a flexible workforce (casual, temporary workers, contract workers and homeworkers) in order to achieve just-in-time ordering, seasonal fluctuations in orders and prices, and competition driving costs down among suppliers (Fair Wear Foundation 2018a, 2018b; Morris & Pillinger 2016). Many work in subcontracted enterprises, beyond the reach of the corporate social responsibility policies on sourcing practices of lead companies (Dejardin 2008; Staritz & Reis 2013). Where there is subcontracting, jobs are typically insecure, wages are low, and working conditions are poor (Barrientos 2001).

In this context, collective bargaining in complex global supply chains is extremely difficult. In global supply chains, social dialogue has helped to secure improvements in productivity, safe work practices and respect for workers' rights, limits on excessive working hours and improved work organization (ILO 2016a; Morris & Pillinger 2016). In the IFC/ILO Better Work programme, which aims to improve conditions in factories in the garment supply chain, social dialogue has proved extremely important. Access to independent workers' organizations has empowered women and given them the voice to represent their interests in the workplace. Interviews with over 15,000 garment workers and 2,000 factory managers in Haiti, Indonesia, Jordan, Nicaragua and Vietnam (Better Work 2013, 2015) show women workers are earning higher wages and now work in a more dignified working environment with reduced incidents of sexual harassment. A further way unions have addressed this issue is through global framework agreements.

GLOBAL FRAMEWORK AGREEMENTS (GFAS)

GFAs, also known as international framework agreements, have the broad objective to promote compliance with international labour standards in the countries where MNEs operate. GFAs are a framework for social dialogue between companies and trade unions on freedom of association, collective bargaining and respect for workers' rights, where these do not exist or need to be strengthened at the national level.

GFAs have enabled GUFs to build international cooperation, joint action, and global solidarity among trade unions across different countries where the MNE operates (Hadwiger 2015). GFAs are qualitatively different from codes of conduct or other voluntary initiatives as they are the outcome of negotiations with global union organizations and constitute a formal recognition of an agreement at global level to protect trade union rights and encourage social dialogue and collective bargaining. They complement and reinforce but do not substitute for collective agreements at the national or local level. GFAs therefore are an entry point for unions to organize, gain recognition and bargaining rights and to start a social dialogue with the company, its subcontractors and suppliers. GFAs are underpinned by a number of non-binding international instruments concerning business operations, which are summarized in the box below.

BUSINESS AND HUMAN RIGHTS INITIATIVES

The ILO Tripartite Declaration of Principles concerning Multinational Enterprises and Social Policy (MNE Declaration) was adopted in 1977 and last revised in 2017. As a tripartite negotiated instrument, it provides an authoritative set of principles that promotes both fundamental rights and a broad range of good industrial relations practices.

The UN Guiding Principles on Business and Human Rights adopted in 2011 is based on three pillars of the state's duty to protect against human rights abuses by third parties; the business responsibility to respect human rights and the victims' rights to effective remedies. While they considerably extend the scope and responsibility for business operations to respect human rights, they are non-binding. There is currently a new UN initiative to establish a legally binding treaty and for that purpose, the Human Rights Council established an open-ended working group on transnational corporations and other business enterprises with respect to human rights in 2014.

The OECD Guidelines for Multinational Enterprises were adopted in 1976 and updated in 2011, following the adoption of the UN Guiding Principles. They have been adopted by 42 governments, and spell out government expectations on responsible business conduct, primarily addressed to MNEs based in those countries that adhere to them but concerning their operations wherever they may be. The revised sections particularly concern risk-based due diligence and responsible supply chain management. The guidelines are supported by implementation procedures where the ultimate responsibility for their enforcement lies with governments that must establish national contact points (NCPs), which provide mediation and conciliation services. This makes the guidelines the only international corporate responsibility instrument with a built-in grievance mechanism, which can be used by trade unions and other civil society organizations.

The number of GFAs has grown from 61 GFAs in 2007 to 115 signed in 2016 (ILO 2018e), with the majority having headquarters in Europe (Stevis 2010). GFAs are principally found in the private sector, and many are in male-dominated industries, such as mining, building, chemical and car manufacturing. However, in recent years there has been an increase in the number of GFAs in sectors that employ large numbers of women, for example, in textiles, clothing, retail and horticulture. In the past, the monitoring mechanisms of GFAs have been relatively weak, and more recent GFAs have strengthened these aspects (ILO 2018f).

To date, there has been no detailed analysis carried out of the gender equality provisions in GFAs and therefore of the future implications of progressing regional or global collective bargaining on gender equality issues. Pillinger's (2017b) review for the ILO found that around one-quarter of GFAs refer to harassment, sexual harassment and/or dignity at work but often in very general ways, with very few including concrete and detailed provisions for workplace procedures to address violence and harassment.

In practice, most agreements refer to adherence to fundamental rights and ILO core labour standards: freedom of association, collective bargaining, equal remuneration and non-discrimination, abolition of forced labour, and elimination of child labour. Some GFAs also include minimum terms and conditions of employment, some of which are important gender equality issues (working hours, wages, health and safety, equal pay, maternity rights, violence and harassment, amongst others). Most GFAs refer specifically to ILO Convention 100 on equal remuneration, ILO Convention 111 on non-discrimination, and some refer to ILO Convention 183 on maternity protection and ILO Convention 156 on workers with family responsibilities, while a few refer to CEDAW Convention article 11 on employment, and some GFAs address gender-based violence at the workplace. Given the practice of adherence to principles and obligations set out in existing international labour standards, the proposed ILO labour standard on violence and harassment against women and men in the world of work will provide a framework for obligations on this issue to be included in future GFAs.

Some agreements contain specific clauses related to harassment and violence, as is the case of the GFA between Faber-Castell and BWI (2008), which states that "(p)hysical abuse, the threat of physical abuse, unusual penalties or punishments, sexual or other forms of harassment and threats by the employer shall be strictly forbidden". This is also the case with the GFA between the European Aeronautic Defence and Space Company (EADS) and EMF (2005); agreement on "Diversity" between IUF and Danone (2007); the IUF-Unilever agreement (2016); and the GFA signed between GDF and EPSU/IndustriALL Europe (2014). Examples of GFAs covering female-dominated sectors can be found in the box below.

GLOBAL FRAMEWORK AGREEMENTS/JOINT COMMITMENTS THAT ADDRESS GENDER EQUALITY

The GFA between Inditex and IndustriALL global union on the "implementation of international labour standards throughout the supply chain of Inditex", signed in 2007 and renewed in 2014, was the first agreement to address precarious work in the garment supply chain, particularly in complex subcontracting arrangements (Inditex and IndustriALL 2014). It covers one million, predominantly women, garment workers both home-based and in over 6,000 factories worldwide. IndustriAll estimates that 90 per cent of workers in the global garment industry are not covered by industry wage bargaining, but instead are reliant on minimum wage-setting mechanisms that are often ineffective. The revised Inditex agreement in 2014 includes new standards aimed at strengthening the scope and reach of the GFA, including effective monitoring. Suppliers and contractors are covered under the provisions: suppliers accept responsibility for subcontractor compliance and no subcontracting is allowed without the prior consent of Inditex. In addition to the principled reference to the fundamental ILO conventions, including Convention 100 on equal remuneration and Convention 111 on non-discrimination, it provides for a living wage for a standard working week, limitations on working hours, and health and safety provisions in the workplace. Crucially, suppliers accept responsibility for subcontractor compliance. The review and monitoring mechanisms are also strengthened and there are provisions for training programmes for management and workers. A Joint Understanding was negotiated within the gender subcommittee of the review committee under the framework agreement and includes a Code of Conduct prohibiting forced labour, child labour, discrimination and harsh and inhumane treatment throughout the Inditex supply chain. The Code of Conduct applies on an equal basis to direct suppliers, contractors and subcontractors, including homeworkers.

In 2013, Hennes and Mauritz developed one of the first publicly disclosed living wage roadmaps and was a signatory to the new ACT initiative in 2015 with IndustriALL, to address collective bargaining in low-wage countries for garment production, starting in Cambodia (Oxfam 2018). A GFA between Hennes and Mauritz GBC AB and IndustriALL and IF Metall (the Swedish union) was signed in 2015, protecting the interests of 1.6 million garment workers (Hennes and Mauritz, IndustriALL, IF Metall 2015). The GFA covers compliance with and implementation of international labour standards by the Hennes and Mauritz suppliers, including the right to organize and to negotiate collective agreements and non-discrimination. A grievance mechanism has been put in place to enable workers to make complaints without retaliation.

A GFA that is proactive on gender equality is the Carrefour–UNI GFA first signed in 2001, and updated in 2015 and 2018 (Carrefour–UNI 2015 and 2018). It covers one of the world's largest retail distribution groups, made up of hypermarkets, supermarkets, cash and carry wholesalers and convenience stores across the world. The GFA contains a strong gender equality focus and also references CEDAW and the UN's women's empowerment principles. The preparation of the agreement involved information and training sessions within the Carrefour European Information and Consultation Committee for Equality between Men and Women (CICE), a bipartite management-union committee on gender equality. The provisions introduced in 2015 refer to a safe, healthy and respectful working environment, including the prevention of psychosocial risks, anti-discrimination and the promotion of diversity and equality between women and men. The 2018 renewal includes, among other areas, provisions relating to violence against women at work.

Commitments include an annual survey of "the place of women in the Group's structures" based on a set of indicators on hiring, training, career promotion, remuneration, working conditions and work–life balance to be reviewed by the CICE. The objectives are to increase the representation of women at managerial level, equal opportunities in hiring and promotion, support for pregnant and nursing women, with adjustments to hours and working conditions and staff returning from maternity or paternity leave. Measures to enable better work–life balance include reference to good prac-tice, training for management, measures to allow parents to support children during illness or in their education, and encouraging parenting among male employees. The agreement also provides for the development of guidance tools to support these measures. The GFA requests that franchise operators sign the Carrefour charter for commitment to respect human rights, based on the ILO's conventions on fundamental labour rights.

The GFA between the Italian energy company ENEL and IndustriAll, PSI, FILTCEM CGIL, FLAEI CISL, and UILTEC UIL (2014), includes a commit-ment to social dialogue and good global industrial relations, as well as to gender equality and non-discrimination. A global works council has been established across the group, with the aim of monitoring implementation and ENEL has made a commitment to roll-out the best initiatives in this area across all group companies and through the establishment of a multilateral committee on equal opportunities.

Some GUFs provide specific guidance on integrating gender equality issues into global framework agreements and monitor the content of agreements to ensure that gender equality issues are included as obligations. For example, UNI global union has drawn up a model equality clause for inclusion in GFAs, on the right to non-discrimination, equal opportunities and treatment for women and under-represented groups, right to equal pay for work of equal value and the fight to reconcile professional life with family responsibilities. The model equality clause has already been included in many GFAs, including those agreed with Carrefour, ABN AMRO, ITAU, and Société Génerale. The BWI global union also has a model GFA that includes provisions on equality and non-discrimination, although the focus is most particularly on the rights of migrant workers, particularly in the case of contract workers. A recent development is the signing of agreements with detailed sections or annexes on sexual harassment at work, see the box below.

AGREEMENTS/JOINT COMMITMENTS WITH DETAILED SECTIONS ON THE ISSUE OF SEXUAL HARASSMENT

The IUF, IndustriAll and Unilever "Joint Commitment to preventing sexual harassment" (IUF, IndustriAll & Unilever 2016) also addresses workforce diversity. It includes a joint commitment to promoting diversity and inclusion within Unilever's non-management workforce. It emphasizes that "(p)reventing sexual harassment in the workplace is an essential foundation for promoting a culture of inclusion and diversity" and "full protection and support is given to the victims of sexual harassment throughout the process and its outcome". It goes further than most agreements by stating that in situations where there are significant risks faced by women workers, for example, in plantations employing large numbers of temporary labour and where there are high numbers of females supervised by a majority of males, "specific awareness and training measures should be agreed and deployed by management and the trade union". A Unilever–IUF–IndustriAll Joint Working Group on Diversity has been established to monitor the process and share experiences and best practices. The agreement builds on work carried out to raise awareness of gender inequalities, as part of Unilever's goal for gender balance in every workplace.

Sodexo, the French food services and facilities management company, which claims to be the world's nineteenth largest employer, has worked with the IUF to develop measures to address sexual harassment. An annex to the existing GFA was agreed in 2018 known as the "SODEXO-IUF Joint

Commitment on preventing sexual harassment" (SODEXO-IUF 2018). This commitment spells out the principle that there should be zero tolerance by Sodexo, the IUF and its affiliates for sexual harassment; that it is an offence which can lead to a disciplinary penalty, including dismissal from the company; and that Sodexo will provide training for all staff on this policy and their responsibilities under it. Sodexo also undertook to include a clause prohibiting sexual harassment in its supplier code of conduct, to inform its subcontractors and suppliers of this policy and to use its influence to resolve any case of sexual harassment that might arise. IUF has produced a guidebook for trade unions "Zero tolerance for sexual harassment at Sodexo", setting out action for unions to take to implement the agreement (IUF undated).

GFAs represent a transnational form of collective bargaining but they are not easy to implement in countries that have weak regulation of freedom of association and collective bargaining. The more recent GFAs have established joint worker–employer monitoring committees not just in direct employment of the MNE, but also in supply chain contracting arrangements. For example, the Hennes and Mauritz–IndustriALL agreement led to the creation of a global monitoring committee and national monitoring committees in Bangladesh, Indonesia, Myanmar and Turkey, with the aim to support negotiations between employers' and workers' organizations at the factory level. In Cambodia, the agreement has helped to ensure that garment workers receive minimum wages and other rights, which had been denied them. However, research has also revealed problems with suppliers not paying minimum wages, or denying women sick leave or toilet breaks, and regular reports of workers fainting in the heat (Asia Wage Floor Alliance *et. al.* 2018; Preston & Leffler 2016).

The Inditex/IndustriALL agreement has also set up similar monitoring arrangements. As a result of the GFA, the concept of a living wage was introduced into Inditex's code of conduct on the basis that: "wages should always be enough to meet at least the basic needs of workers and their families and any other which might be considered as reasonable additional needs". Joint IndustriALL and Inditex training projects in Turkey, Morocco, Brazil, Portugal, Argentina and China have helped to establish worker–management negotiations in factories. The new revised agreement, signed in 2016, designated union experts within the retail group's supplier clusters (in Spain, Portugal, Morocco, Turkey, Vietnam, Cambodia, Bangladesh, India, Argentina, Brazil and China) to monitor, supervise and accompany its suppliers worldwide.

EUROPEAN AND OTHER REGIONAL FRAMEWORK AGREEMENTS

European framework agreements are the most common form of regional agreement. They are a key component of the "European social model" and take place at two levels: through the cross-sectoral and sectoral social dialogue and at company level through European works councils. European social dialogue is formally recognized by the Treaty on the Functioning of the European Union (articles 154 and 155) as a fundamental part of the European social model. An example is the 2015–17 "Partnership for inclusive growth and employment", which includes "reconciliation of work, private and family life and gender equality" as one of eight priority areas.

At the cross-sectoral European level, four framework agreements have been agreed between the social partners and implemented by Council directives. They include the parental leave directive (1996), a revised and extended parental leave directive (2009) providing four months parental leave, one month of which is non-transferable between parents; the part-time work directive (1997); and the directive on fixed-term contracts (1999). There are also "autonomous" agreements, whereby the social partners themselves take responsibility for implementing measures at national, sectoral and enterprise level. They include agreements on telework (2002), work-related stress (2004), harassment and violence at work (2007) and inclusive labour markets (2010). A further and significant achievement is the European social partners framework of actions on gender equality (ETUC *et al.* 2005), where the member organizations of the BUSINESSEUROPE, UEAPME, CEEP and ETUC agreed to focus on four areas for priority actions (address gender roles; promote women in decision-making; support work–life balance; and tackle the gender pay gap). The 2009 evaluation cited many examples of how national social partners implemented the framework of actions through collective bargaining, positive actions and awareness raising (ETUC *et al.* 2009). In May 2014, the European cross-industry social partners launched a web-based tool: "A toolkit for gender equality in practice", which highlights 100 innovative initiatives by social partners in different sectors and across Europe (BUSINESSEUROPE, UEAPME, CEEP & ETUC 2014).

European social dialogue committees, first established in 1985, have concluded almost 300 joint texts, which include joint opinions and agreements, guidelines and codes of conduct in different sectors of the economy. By 2015, 43 sectoral social dialogue committees had been established, each with a work programme jointly agreed between the social partners. Many of the sectoral European trade union federations have policies and projects with employers to promote gender equality at a sectoral level (European Commission 2010, 2012, 2014; ILO 2013a). EPSU has carried out the most extensive work in this area with a specific focus on equal pay, based on its 2009 congress resolution, which reaffirmed a target for its affiliates "of reducing the gender pay gap by at least 5 per cent by 2014". In addition, EPSU equal pay surveys reveal the difficulties affiliates face in addressing this issue, although there are some positive developments in social dialogue at the European level in the public sector (EPSU 2013).

EXAMPLES OF EUROPEAN SOCIAL DIALOGUE INITIATIVES ON GENDER EQUALITY

Two sectoral agreements specifically concern female-dominated sectors. An agreement on the implementation of the European hairdressing certificates was signed on 18 June 2009 by the European social partners and a framework agreement on prevention from sharp injuries in the hospitals and healthcare sector was concluded by HOSPEEM and EPSU and implemented as Council Directive 2010/32/EU of 10 May 2010.

The Council of European Municipalities and Regions (CEMR) and EPSU adopted guidelines on drawing up equality action plans in 2007, which were updated in 2017.

The European social dialogue committee for Central Government Administrations held detailed discussions about the gender pay gap. In 2014, TUNED (Trade Unions' National and European Delegation) and EUPAE (European Public Administration Employers) adopted "Recommendations towards closing the gender pay gap".

The European social dialogue committee on Telecommunications, with the social partners UNI Europa and the European Telecommunication Network Operators' Association (ETNO) signed a joint declaration on gender equality in 2014.

The European Transport Federation (ETF) and the Community of European Railway and Infrastructure Companies (CER) joint actions include a survey on women's employment in the railway sector in 2014 and a project between the social partners in urban transport, ETF and the International Association of Public Transport (UITP), resulted in joint guidelines and recommendation on strengthening women's employment in the sector. On the basis of the ETF (2017) research on violence against women in the transport sector, recommendations were discussed with European transport employers in relevant social dialogue committees with a view to drawing up concrete social dialogue initiatives to prevent violence and harassment against women. In 2018, the European social partners in the shipping sector held a joint social dialogue workshop on "Women and Shipping", building on the joint ETF and European Community Shipowners' Association (ECSA) project on the eradication of harassment and bullying in shipping, leading to the development of a training video and workbook.

European works councils (EWCs) have incorporated gender issues into a number of European framework agreements at company level. The establishment of EWCs dates back to 1994 (Directive 94/45/EC) and a recast directive was adopted in 2009 (Directive 2009/38/EC). The ETUI's database of EWCs has over 1,000 active EWCs covering all major sectors of the economy.

One landmark EWC agreement is the EPSU/IndustriALL/GDF-Suez European agreement on professional equality (GDF-Suez Group 2012). Commitment is made for the progressive reduction of pay discrepancies and to eliminate any pay gaps at the point of recruitment, to ensure that maternity leave does not have negative consequences on salaries or career development; measures to facilitate work–life balance and to ensure that taking paternity leave and parental leave by men is regarded as normal and desirable; and policies to prevent sexual harassment. The agreement established a commission with 50 per cent women tasked with carrying out an annual review of progress based on a set of detailed indicators.

Framework agreements from regions other than Europe are not common. However, they are becoming more important in the context of global supply chains that focus on company-wide rather than sector-wide issues. An example of a regional framework agreement is given below from Latin America, which represents one of the first agreements with a gender focus in response to the need to tackle gender inequalities and high levels of sexual harassment in the banana sector in Latin America.

IUF/COLSIBA AND CHIQUITA BANANA COMPANY

The Chiquita Banana Company and IUF/COLSIBA-Latin American agreed a landmark regional framework agreement in 2001 following several years of coordinated union/NGO advocacy, led by the IUF and the coordinating body of Latin American Banana and Agro-industrial Unions (COLSIBA). The agreement also covers suppliers, contract growers and joint ventures. The banana sector in Latin America employs large numbers of women; and violence against women, and particularly sexual harassment is very prevalent. In 2013, the IUF and COLSIBA signed a new appendix to the regional framework agreement that commits the parties to: "developing a joint understanding on sexual harassment, so that this kind of harassment will not be tolerated in the workplace". There is also a provision to work on "training strategies and sharing examples of good practice" and recognition that "every workplace must take necessary measures to ensure men and women workers have access to information about their rights in the workplace". The new appendix references the ILO code of practice on safety and health in agriculture, for language on prevention of sexual harassment that could be included in CBAs at national and local levels. The appendix was negotiated in the gender subcommittee of the framework's review committee.

CONCLUSION

Global framework agreements, cross-sectoral and sectoral regional and company agreements are important mechanisms to monitor the implementation of ILO labour standards, and to promote decent working conditions in global supply chains and in EPZs, many of which employ a predominantly female workforce. Although there are many challenges in establishing effective enforcement mechanisms, transnational social dialogue and bargaining with MNEs has the potential to benefit some of the most exploited women workers in developing countries. In recent years GFAs covering female-dominated sectors, such as garments and horticulture, have sought to tackle the profound gender inequalities at work, and more recently address workplace cultures of high levels of sexual harassment and abuse.

These GFAs have given significant leverage to unions organizing workers in supplier factories or farms, and provide avenues for unions to report non-compliance to global monitoring committees and helplines, while also raising awareness of the importance of union organizing with the workforce. In the export-orientated horticultural sector, unions have successfully mobilized to secure agreements strengthening workers' protections and including the promotion of gender equality in the workplace and prevention of sexual harassment (Morris & Pillinger 2016). Hadwiger's (2015a, 2015b) review of 29 case studies of GFAs concludes that there are good practices of effective coordination between suppliers, subcontractors and subsidiaries and the strengthening of international solidarity between unions across national borders.

In some cases, as part of multi-stakeholder initiatives such as the Fair Wear Foundation, the Ethical Trading Initiative, and Clean Clothes Campaign, unions, brands and companies have also adopted commitments to implement fundamental labour standards, living wages and gender equality programmes across their supply chains, and to carry out regular audits with their suppliers on their implementation. These initiatives are having an impact on working conditions for women garment workers in Bangladesh, India, Indonesia, Vietnam and Cambodia, including addressing excessive overtime, low wages and a culture of sexual harassment (Fair Wear Foundation 2018b).

In Europe, social dialogue at a sectoral and cross-sectoral level, in part a result of the stronger union–employer bargaining systems compared to other parts of the world, and a strong representation of women in some sectors, has been reinforced by the EU's commitment to social dialogue and gender equality.

In conclusion, this review of GFAs identifies a trend of a clear progression in the scope and detail of gender equality clauses, with commitments to extend the agreements throughout the supply chain and to improve monitoring mechanisms. Recent innovations include clauses related to gender-based violence, which have perhaps been more easily negotiated as the cost outcomes are less than in the case of pay audits to address the gender pay gap or commitments to living wages. Many employers view these agreements as opportunities to establish frameworks for gender equality policies, in areas such as training and promotion of women into management and leadership positions, work–life balance and women's safety and health at work, all of which can also help business profitability, retention of workers and avoidance of reputational damage.

Both the work towards a new legally binding UN treaty on transnational corporations and other business enterprises with respect to human rights (ICJ 2016) and the new ILO standard on violence and harassment against women and men in the world of work (ILO 2018b) will provide strengthened frameworks for due diligence and respect for human rights in business operations throughout the global supply chain, which can be referenced and used to strengthen the monitoring mechanisms of future GFAs.

The major challenge remains to see how far strengthened monitoring provisions in recent GFAs have a real impact on women workers, particularly where subcontracting and home-based work takes place. As the number of GFAs continues to increase, GUFs and their affiliates are giving attention to researching, resourcing and establishing effective monitoring and reporting mechanisms and building alliances with other labour rights organizations, NGOs, and women's organizations to tackle income inequalities and labour abuses, with a strong gender and diversity perspective.

6

Conclusion

Collective bargaining, as both a tool for representing workers' interests and a method for finding common solutions with employers to workplace issues, has enormous potential to address structural gender inequalities. However, many of the changes discussed in this book point to the need for new thinking about how gender equality can be more effectively integrated into union strategies, policies and advocacy. Both bipartite and tripartite social dialogue has never been so relevant to workers, particularly to women workers in formal and informal employment across the world. At the International Labour Conference in 2009, tripartite delegations discussing "gender equality at the heart of decent work" emphasized that social dialogue is fundamentally about equitable participation.

> It is through participation that women and men can achieve decent and productive work in conditions of freedom, equity, security and human dignity ... The challenges of promoting gender equality through social dialogue are twofold. First, there is the matter of increasing the participation and status of women in the process. Second, there is the challenge of introducing a gender perspective into the content so as to reflect the changing nature of labour markets and patterns in the world of work. (ILO 2009a: 161)

These same issues were still being discussed in 2018 at the ILC, where a resolution on social dialogue and tripartism stressed the urgency of ensuring that social dialogue addresses gender equality in the light of the rapidly changing world of work (ILO 2018g). Women have entered paid employment and are joining unions or other membership-based organizations in growing numbers, and in some countries, women now outnumber men in union membership. However, in many parts of the world, collective bargaining coverage continues to be limited and only covers a proportion of the formal economy workforce, often in male-dominated industries and the public sector. Collective agreements do not necessarily extend to contract and subcontracted workers in the supply chain in key sectors of women's employment. The majority of workers, many of whom are women own-account workers in the informal economy, remain outside of and are unprotected by collective bargaining. This book has sought to explore how collective bargaining on gender equality can remain relevant when the vast majority of largely unorganized informal workers have little or no trade union representation or bargaining power.

A key theme to emerge in this book is the importance of the political context, including national institutional settings, industrial relations systems and social security regimes (Fuchs 2010), and the extent to which countries engage in social dialogue and create an enabling legal environment for collective bargaining. There are difficulties in some contexts of preserving equality gains that result from varying levels of institutional support. Despite austerity measures, budget reductions on equality institutions and the lower priority given in some countries to gender equality in legislation – and to human rights and the rule of law generally – collective bargaining still remains one of several mechanisms that has potential to promote and achieve equality.

The following are the most important dynamics that can impact on whether collective bargaining promotes equality:

- Respect for the fundamental rights to freedom of association and collective bargaining.
- The role of legislation to support the integration of gender equality issues into the collective bargaining process, by providing incentives for both unions and employers to address key gender equality issues, including gender mainstreaming.

- Collective bargaining structures and the degree of centralization and coordination of bargaining, which also allows for local innovation.
- The role of trade union and employer internal and external policies on gender equality, taking into account women's multiple and intersecting forms of discrimination.
- The extent to which women participate in leadership and decision-making positions, including in collective bargaining teams, and their relative influence on forms and styles of negotiation.
- Consultation mechanisms and civil society alliances to ensure that woman's voice, agency and interests are reflected in collective bargaining agendas and negotiations.
- The extent to which the scope of collective bargaining adapts to globalization and extends into global supply chains.

The book has identified two main developments in collective bargaining in the promotion of equality. First, there is a range of ways in which a gender-perspective has been integrated into mainstream bargaining agendas, with positive implications for gender equality in the workplace, principally around wages, working time, job security and working conditions. These developments have led to the removal of overtly discriminatory provisions in collective agreements and in job classification schemes, as well as the overall recognition that the traditional breadwinner model of bargaining is no longer relevant in many countries, given the extent of dual-earning households. Second, a broader range of specific gender issues is now included in CBAs. This broadening of the collective bargaining agenda has led to a more systematic approach to addressing gender inequalities and understanding the intersecting forms of discrimination faced by women workers, progressed in areas such as equal pay for work for equal value, maternity protection, reconciliation of work and family life and more recently gender-based violence. There is now a much higher priority afforded to the issue of how to address women's disproportionate share of care responsibilities and increased attention to the impact of domestic violence in the workplace.

This book has looked at the added value of collective bargaining to gender equality, recognizing that by itself it cannot achieve gender equality goals but must be set in a context of social, political reforms and cultural change. CBAs create fairer workplaces, which bring gender benefits, and they address other forms of discrimination, help to achieve other gains such as enhanced productivity or improved services, as well as being an important tool for conflict resolution.

Collective bargaining can also allow more flexibility than legislation, particularly as CBAs are renewed on a regular basis and they include a cost effective individual grievance mechanism. Further, it is empowering as it informs and engages workers on issues of direct concern to them. A further advantage is that CBAs and GFAs can be extended to cover workers through the supply chains, lending the bargaining power of formal sector workers to workers in precarious situations, including home-based workers.

There has been little research to monitor the outcomes of CBAs and GFAs from a gender perspective, and the overall impact of gender equality provisions in collective agreements in practice. Further research is needed at national, regional and global levels to systematically analyze both the content of agreements and their outcomes in relation to gender equality. Key questions include: How effectively are gender equality provisions in collective agreements implemented? What are the obstacles that women workers face when they seek to realize their rights laid down in collective agreements and how can these obstacles be overcome? To what extent are other labour institutions, such as the labour inspectorate or labour court judges, implementing a gender equality perspective in their work or are there capacity gaps that need to be addressed? How effective are the social and economic institutions that have a complementary role to play in monitoring gender equality outcomes in CBAs, including the role of government equality bodies?

THE IMPORTANCE OF STRONG LEGAL FRAMEWORKS AND NATIONAL/SECTORAL BARGAINING

While legislation can provide an enabling framework, CBAs are the most effective mechanism to monitor, enforce and advance legislative gains on equality. In best practice, the two work together in a complementary "partnership". Collective bargaining in addressing gender pay inequalities is considerably strengthened when legislation spells out obligations on the social partners to draw up equality initiatives in the workplace, resulting in unions and employers becoming more actively engaged. The importance of strong laws as incentives for unions and employers to negotiate, and that place duties on employers, for example, on pay transparency, are particularly important. The strong support for an ILO convention on violence and harassment against women and men in the world of work is also evidence of the need for robust laws, prevention programmes, and workplace measures to end violence against women and men at work (ILO 2018b).

Collective bargaining also has been used to reinforce and extend legal norms as set out in international labour standards and national equality legislation. Those countries with well-established rights to collective bargaining also share strong legal commitments to gender equality. There needs to be strong and sustained pressure, including legal obligations, by multilateral organizations, such as the ILO, the UN, international development organizations and international development banks, on states and MNEs across global supply chains, to promote respect of freedom of association and the right to collective bargaining.

GENDER EQUALITY AND UNION RENEWAL: THE CONTINUING CHALLENGE

On an internal level, unions have shifted from representing occupational categories and interests of predominantly male workers, and have adopted new organizing and recruitment strategies, reflecting the increasingly diverse and feminized workforce and membership. However, union structures and leadership have been less willing to represent proportionally this diverse and female membership. In some unions and in some countries, women are increasingly participating in leadership but the pace of change needs to be dramatically up-scaled. In addition, unions need to include organizations of informal workers, such as local associations and cooperatives, in rule-setting, policy-making and collective bargaining.

Significantly, unions have found they can no longer accommodate "women's issues" into collective bargaining without changing existing structures and leadership. For example, although garment workers in some Asian countries have secured important gains, many of the unions remain patriarchal and authoritarian (Evans 2017). Unions that fail to address these issues will remain weak, non-representative and they will be unable to build strong alliances with women and civil society organizations in the wider community. Ensuring that women are in decision-making positions and that there is gender-balanced representation on collective bargaining teams and elsewhere needs to be reinforced and strengthened. There is also a need to increase coordination between collective bargaining and gender equality units within unions, and effective integration of transformational gender mainstreaming. In addition, while measures to improve minimum wages are important for low-paid women workers, gender-specific measures are also needed to address the undervaluing of women's work, to develop transparent pay systems and to extend duties on employers to actively promote this approach.

Throughout the book, many good practices illustrate ways in which collective bargaining has been transformed; however, in many cases they remain the exception rather than the rule. The economic crisis and austerity measures, as well as having devastating effects on women's employment and pay, showed the fragility of the gender equality consensus in collective bargaining, as gender issues slipped off bargaining agendas in some countries. Nevertheless, there are many examples in the ETUC's Europe-wide survey "Bargaining for Equality" (Pillinger 2014) pointing to the importance given by unions to the goal of gender equality and the surprising resilience – and subsequent resurgence – of collective bargaining in some countries. While progress is slow, the survey pointed to a number of successes arising from increasing feminization of unions (where women now comprise about 45 per cent of ETUC membership); evidence of a greater priority given to gender equality in union policies and strategies; and the introduction of gender-mainstreaming approaches in collective bargaining in some unions. There are also

good examples of trade union manuals, model clauses and training programmes on gender-mainstreaming, setting out negotiating agendas in
pay bargaining, working hours and flexible work, and violence and harassment against women at work.

While these represent good practice developments in trade unions,
there is a need for further tools to carry out gender impact assessments
at all stages of collective bargaining so as to methodically test whether
bargaining is gender neutral or whether the outcomes of agreements
have unintended negative gender impacts. In this regard, unions should
be encouraged to adopt gender mainstreaming strategies and guidelines
that set out criteria for carrying out gender impact assessments of CBAs,
their impact and effectiveness.

Similarly, unions can play an enabling role in providing regular
training courses and guidance for negotiators, officials and workplace
representatives on gender mainstreaming, gender-neutral criteria for
bargaining, what to include in negotiations and how to bargain around
different topics ranging from the reduction of gender inequalities in
pay to sexual harassment at work. Gender mainstreaming tools for bargaining teams need to include topics such as gender-neutral job evaluation and job classification, and methodologies to address underlying
and structural causes of inequality, including occupational segregation,
low pay, undervaluing of women's work and women's burden of care
work; and how to effectively integrate gender equality considerations
into occupational safety and health programmes. There is a need to
strengthen the capacity of works councils and workplace committees to
enable them to understand pay transparency, interpret pay reports and
monitor implementation of measures designed to reduce the gender pay
gap. There are also attitudinal changes which need to be encouraged,
with styles of negotiation moving away from brinkmanship, confron-
tation and all-night sessions, to more gender-friendly and collaborative
processes, which can also help facilitate women's participation in collective bargaining.

The lack of pay transparency and particularly of gender-disaggregated
data on pay severely impedes the capacity of unions and employers to
negotiate to tackle increasing wage dispersion and reduce the gender pay

gap. A positive development in the last five years has been the emphasis in both legislation and on negotiations for mandatory pay reports on gender pay gaps, and ensuring that both union representatives and equality bodies have access to these reports. Unions in some countries have played a very proactive role in this regard. However, unions could more forcefully advocate for employers and in some instances key government departments to be provided with guidance and training on the concepts of equal pay for work of equal value as there is still considerable misunderstanding and ambiguity surrounding these terms.

Another key area is the promotion of job evaluation and classification systems as the use of job evaluation outside the public sector is still relatively limited. Where job classification systems do exist, they need to be carefully scrutinized to identify any possible gender bias. Some unions have advocated for public procurement policies to provide incentives for companies to address the gender pay gap, as a response to higher levels of contracting out and commercialization in the public sector.

BROADENING THE COLLECTIVE BARGAINING AGENDA

New issues are coming onto union and collective bargaining agendas that focus on women in precarious work and that connect work–family life. There are innovative forms of bargaining for women in low-paid jobs, for example, that are advocating for increased coverage and enforcement of adequate minimum wage floors and the expansion of social protection coverage for all, according to principles of equity and sustainability.

In terms of work–life balance, there are now better incentives for men to take paid parental leave and thus promote the equal sharing of care responsibilities, as has been achieved in Sweden. Non-transferable leave entitlements for mothers and fathers, flexible work choices and other gender diverse and family-friendly working arrangements are also increasingly integrated into collective bargaining agendas. These measures are combined with advocacy for enhanced State provision or support for childcare and elderly care. In the area of health and safety at work, some unions have drawn up checklists that integrate gender equality issues, as is the case of the STUC, the TUC and Unite in the UK. Psychosocial harassment, stress and violence at work have become more important workplace issues and are featuring more regularly on safety and health committee agendas, risk assessments and company safety and health policies, which have proved the entry point for new issues such as gender-based violence, including domestic violence at work (ILO 2018b; Moore 2018; Pillinger 2017a).

NEW PROTECTION FOR PRECARIOUS AND INFORMAL WORKERS

Some of the most innovative and ground-breaking work arises from new organizing and recruitment strategies, reflecting an increasingly diverse and feminized workforce, that have emerged to protect precarious and informal workers. These include networks developed with NGOs, representation mechanisms such as informal workers' committees in trade unions, or bargaining forums in which trade unions participate alongside informal workers' organizations. Trade unions have also advocated for reforms to legal frameworks so as to provide protection to informal workers and their livelihoods. Extending legal recognition to informal workers can in the first instance be achieved through relatively simple measures such as the provision of identity cards recognizing their profession and classifying them as workers. Another area is to provide legal protection in the form of enforceable contracts or property rights. Other measures include the extension of minimum wage requirements, health and safety regulations, social security and other labour rights to informal workers, including those employed through contractors or other intermediaries and on-call and temporary workers. The organizing work carried out by trade unions and civil society organizations, often in partnership, is an interesting and new approach to bargaining, that reflects new possibilities for the future whereby bargaining principally takes place with local authorities or other entities, rather than employers.

INTERSECTIONALITY

The structural and enduring nature of gender inequalities, which are compounded by the intersection of race, ethnicity, disability, migrant status, sexual orientation and other forms of discrimination, can only partially be addressed through collective bargaining. While collective bargaining increasingly reflects intersectionality, legal and human rights frameworks, along with public duties on employers, are equally important. Furthermore, as the collective bargaining process has become more complex, negotiators need to understand the interplay of increasingly fragmented employment patterns, the growth of non-standard forms of employment, involuntary part-time work and temporary work from a gender and intersectional perspective. A key challenge at national, regional and international levels is how to develop a framework that recognizes gendered and intersectional inequalities and responds to both business objectives and wider societal needs.

A positive development is that many unions across the world are increasingly addressing intersectional interests (Parker & Douglas 2010; Pillinger 2017b). This approach has resulted in "a critique of power relations in trade unions originating from patriarchal and racialized nation states and institutions, and resulting in multiple systems of discrimination which intersect to reproduce power" (Pillinger 2017b: 10). It has helped women in unions to identify and name discrimination, and discrimination-related violence in the workplace.

We need to build on the intersectional approach to gender equality. This is critical to supporting unions in their future renewal; it is not a technical exercise, but a transformative approach to trade union democracy and to making equitable decisions. We need to look at how we share power and to ensure at least 50/50 women and men in decision-making. A new gender contract needs to deal with the injustices and inequalities by gender at three levels: at the level of employers, trade unions and governments. It must include closing the gender pay gap and the gender pensions gap; transparency and reporting on gender gaps; valuing women's work and women's role in society and in the economy; and a social justice approach through progressive taxation and quality public services.

Gloria Mills, chair of the ETUC's and EPSU's women's committees, speaking at EPSU's European conference for a new gender contract, Prague, February 2018.

GLOBAL RESPONSES TO GLOBAL PROBLEMS

In recent years, global framework agreements (GFAs) have established new bargaining frameworks at a transnational level. However, the monitoring and enforcement mechanisms of GFAs are generally inadequate to ensure the effective right to freedom of association or collective bargaining across all countries where a company operates, or for this to result in extensions of national agreements across subsidiaries and in supply chains. Proposals under discussion at the UN for a binding treaty on business enterprises and human rights have the possibility to significantly strengthen the regulatory frameworks that ensure companies respect and enforce labour rights across their supply chains.

Further innovations, including shifts in bargaining that take account of the increasing prevalence of MNEs are needed. One response to globalization and complex global supply chain problems is the growth of multi-stakeholder initiatives. Organizations such as Fair Wear Foundation, Clean Clothes, the Ethical Trading Initiative, the Ethical Tea Initiative and Banana Link, among others, bring together unions, with employers, lead companies and suppliers, as well as NGOs, to discuss improvements to supply chain working conditions. All have stressed the importance of social dialogue, freedom of association and the right to collective bargaining as fundamental to resolving labour abuses in supply chains.

The learning from the 2013 Rana Plaza factory collapse in Bangladesh, which killed 1,135 (mainly female) garment workers, highlighted the need for workers to be represented by strong unions. The fire led to the recognition of the importance of social dialogue in preventing future tragedies. The Accord on Fire and Building Safety in Bangladesh[7]

---

7. A full copy of the accord (2018 version) can be found at http://bangladeshaccord. org/wp-content/uploads/2018-Accord-full-text.pdf (accessed 24 September 2018).

139

signed between brands, manufacturers and trade unions was a historic, legally binding agreement designed to ensure building and fire safety. The accord covers 200 signatory companies in 1,600 factories, covering 2 million workers. It represents a new model of cooperation between global buyers and trade unions that has shown some progress in improving the safety of workers, although concerns still exist (Prentice & De Neve 2017; Prentice *et al.* 2018). The accord provides a model for innovative solutions to other occupational safety hazards, including violence and harassment against women in the workplace.

Furthermore, global multilateral action to strengthen social dialogue and collective bargaining is increasingly linked to the achievement of the SDGs. Without social dialogue and collective bargaining goal 8 on the attainment of "decent work for all" will remain aspirational, and the achievement of goal 5 on gender equality will be seriously compromised. Further examples of multilateral action include the OECD-ILO "Global Deal for Decent Work and Inclusive Growth", which aims to assist governments, businesses and workers to deliver on the SDGs (OECD 2018) and the ILO-led "Equal Pay International Coalition" (EPIC) involving UN Women and the OECD, in a multi-stakeholder coalition to contribute to the achievement of SDG target 8.5 on equal pay between women and men for work of equal value (ILO 2017b).

MOVING BEYOND EQUALITY BARGAINING
TO GENDER MAINSTREAMING

Gender mainstreaming strategies often adopted by the union women's departments have often been "met with resistance from both employers and vested male union interests" (Fuchs 2010: 1). From a gender-mainstreaming perspective, all CBAs would go through a process of gender-impact assessment and consultations with women workers, beginning with the drawing up of bargaining claims and followed through by gender-balanced negotiating teams; and where negotiations routinely integrate gender concerns so that CBAs are both gender-sensitive and gender-relevant.

Gender-mainstreaming approaches mean that collective bargaining must address structural gender inequalities (direct and indirect discrimination, pay setting and collective bargaining coverage, undervaluing of women's occupations and skills, horizontal and vertical occupational segregation, and assumptions and values based on historic family-wage models). Second, these need to take account of and advocate for the redesigning of the "social" state, through gender-responsive public services and tax justice policies that promote redistribution of resources, funding for universal health and childcare services, social protection floors, amongst others. In this context, collective bargaining must also address the structural inequalities women face in access to paid work, including the impact of women's unpaid care roles and by promoting a genuine work–life balance that recognizes all forms of work, including reproductive, caring, voluntary and "own account" work.

Since the economic crisis trade union strategies in some countries have only maintained rather than progressed measures to promote gender equality. However, there is evidence of on-going debate about how to strengthen collective bargaining and move forward in the current environment. Unions are increasingly discussing visions of a gender-equal society that are transformative and differ from union conversations some decades ago. This discourse recognizes that gender inequalities are harmful to women and men, and to the economy and to society. It places a new value on the participation of women in their unions and the importance of formulating gender-responsive public policies and services. For example, issues concerning women's safety in public spaces when commuting to work or when living in employer-provided accommodation, have broadened union perspectives.

THE NEED FOR NEW AND GENDER-RELEVANT MODELS OF BARGAINING

This book has argued that collective bargaining is a key instrument for the achievement of gender equality, with the potential to contribute to the eradication of persistent gender inequalities in employment and working conditions and the transformation of gender relations generally. However, to do so, unions needs to adopt a more proactive role in influencing policy, setting new objectives and developing innovative models of bargaining that systematically reach out to all women workers.

In some contexts, unions are becoming more closely connected to women's struggles and advocacy in the wider community, arguing that substantive equality will only be achieved if the structural inequalities that span social, economic and workplace domains are addressed. Examples include alliances that link labour and social movements through "community unionism" (Briskin 2014b; McBride & Greenwood 2009). Already in many countries across the world there is evidence of a significant growth of joint union–community campaigns that cover issues such as childcare and violence against women, among others. The ILO describes these developments as a new source of power, often focusing on citizenship rather than labour rights (ILO 2017a). By working with community-based social movements and women's organizations, unions have also found new avenues to increase women members' voice and involvement in union advocacy and negotiations.

Transformations in collective bargaining are beginning to emerge across the world, with some unions, for example representing teachers and nurses, responding to the challenging industrial relations environment with new strategies. For example, teachers' unions have engaged parents and community members in campaigns for quality public education. Healthcare unions have focused on the quality of patient care and patient safety at risk because of low staffing levels and austerity, as well as on pay and conditions of employment. In best practice, new models of collective bargaining can support informal workers in negotiations with municipalities on services, taxes, and relations with police and other enforcement agencies, linking back to the role of trade unions in contributing to wider policy debates on the future of work, access to quality public services, social security or universal basic income. In Canada, for example, these linkages have not only broadened bargaining agendas but has also led to the emergence of women leaders of colour and alliances on community issues (Briskin 2014a, 2014b). WIEGO's recently launched (2017) campaign on quality public childcare services, particularly important for informal women workers, is a further example of how informal workers' organizations and trade unions are collaborating globally.

Trade unions are seeking to adapt to changes in the employment relationship as a result of new information technology (Dau-Schmidt 2007). Increasingly there is a blurring of the employee/employer relation and what constitutes an appropriate bargaining unit, with workers as bogus self-employed, temporary workers or subcontracted workers, and where the real economic power in the relationship resides with a "third party" producer or retailer, in situations of decentralized decision-making. These are issues that are currently being debated in the ILO's Global Commission on the Future of Work (ILO 2017a).

These changes raise important questions about whether collective bargaining strategies need to shift to the setting of minimum standards for all workers, so as to cover workers in precarious work situations and in informal work. Strengthening national and regional tripartite frameworks and social dialogue institutions, enabling unions, employers and governments to negotiate new agreements that have implications for wider gender-relevant economic and social policies is one way forward. Currently in many countries national tripartite social dialogue institutions, such as economic and social councils, have a role in integrating gender issues into negotiations about social and economic policies. For example, the Economic and Social Development Council (CDES) of Brazil was reorganized recently to ensure representation from women, racial groups and different regions (ILO 2018c) and the tripartite councils created in Uruguay have a mandate to promote gender equality (Espino & Pedetti 2012).

A further issue relates to the role of universal basic incomes as a solution to income inequalities and rising poverty and there have been some pilot schemes established in various countries. This would secure basic economic security for everyone, regardless of his or her employment status or means. As argued by Guy Standing (2014) a universal basic income (UBI) would be made available by the state for all adults regardless of whether they work or not. This would constitute a new form of universal social protection that recognizes and values all forms of work, including reproductive, caring, informal and "own account" work. While this has its merits, particularly in taking account of unpaid household labour, UBI in isolation may not necessarily have a gender-equality impact without additional policies that are known to contribute to gender equality such as universal healthcare and quality public education and childcare. Particularly in developing countries, UBI may be counter-productive. For example, Amartya Sen argues that UBI is not the best way to address poverty in India, where funding for healthcare, education, and other public services is deficient, and consequently could lead to the government abdicating responsibility to provide quality public services (Basic Income Earth Network 2017). For this reason, unions may have a bigger impact in advocating for gender-responsive quality public services and wider issues of women's participation in financial and economic decision-making so that gender-sensitive budgeting and planning can be prioritized in the future. Unions might usefully engage further in areas such as the gender-impact of tax policies, and their role in redistribution and in progressing substantive equality.

Finally, it is important to recall that trade unions remain among the largest membership organizations across the world. In the light of the erosion of workers' rights and the "social" state arising from globalization and neoliberalism, there is currently a resurgence of interest in union organizing and representation through collective bargaining. Reversing push-back on gender equality has become urgent. Unions have the capacity to be at the critical edge of new thinking and change and are now debating what shape a transformative gender contract could take in order to respond to twenty-first century workplace issues.

References

3F 2016. Sexchikane Skal Nu Undersøges I Nyt Forskningsprojekt. Available at: http://www.fagbladet3f.dk/temaer/sexchikane/333a52b52de14ceaa580c 1712908f200-20151228-sexchikane-skal-nu-undersoeges-i-nyt-forskning sprojekt (accessed 8 September 2018).

Action Aid 2017. Double Jeopardy: Violence Against Women and Economic Inequality. London: Action Aid.

Addati, L., N. Cassirer & K. Gilchrist 2014. Maternity and Paternity at Work: Law and Practice Across the World. Geneva: International Labour Office.

Aeberhard-Hodges, J. & L. McFerran 2017. "An International Labour Organization instrument on violence against women and men at work: the Australian influence". *Journal of Industrial Relations* 60(2), 246–65.

Akhtar, P. & P. Moore 2017. "The psycho-social impacts of technological change in contemporary workplaces and trade union responses". *International Journal of Labour Research* (forthcoming), special issue edited by A. Biondi & V. Guseva.

Antonczyk, D., B. Fitzenberger & K. Sommerfeld 2010. "Rising wage inequality, the decline of collective bargaining, and the gender wage gap". *Labour Economics* 17(5), 835–47.

Antonopoulos, R. 2009. "The current economic and financial crisis: a gender perspective". Working Paper No. 562. Annandale-on-Hudson: Levy Economic Institute of Bard College.

Antonopoulos, R. & R. Hirway (eds) 2009. *Unpaid Work and the Economy: Gender, Time Use and Poverty*. London: Palgrave Macmillan.

Anxo, D., C. Franz & A. Kummerling 2013. "Working Time and Work–Life Balance in a Life Course Perspective: A Report Based on the Fifth European Working Conditions Survey". Dublin: Eurofound.

Asia Floor Wage Alliance, Central Cambodia, Global Labor Justice, Sedane Labour Resource Centre Indonesia, & Society for Labour and Development

India 2018. "Gender-based violence in H&M garment supply chain: workers voices from the global supply chain". Report to the ILO. Available at: https://www.globallaborjustice.org/hm-afwa-report/ (accessed 8 September 2018).

Baird, M., L. McFerran & I. Wright 2014. "An equality bargaining breakthrough: paid domestic violence leave". *Journal of Industrial Relations* 56(2), 190–207.

Baird, M. & J. Murray 2012. "An analysis of collective bargaining for paid parental leave: sector and context effects". University of Sydney Business School. Available at: http://ilera2012.wharton.upenn.edu/RefereedPapers/BairdMarian%20ILERA.pdf (accessed 8 September 2018).

Barrientos, S. 2001. "Gender, flexibility and global value chains". *IDS Bulletin* 32(3), 83–93.

Berg, J. 2015. "Labour markets, institutions and inequality: building just Societies in the 21st century". Geneva: ILO. Available at: http://www.ilo.org/global/publications/books/WCMS_346629/lang--en/index.htm (accessed 8 September 2018).

Better Work 2013. "Garment factory characteristics and workplace sexual harassment". Research brief. Geneva: ILO. Available at: https://betterwork.org/blog/portfolio/garment-factory-characteristics-and-workplace-sexual-harassment/ (accessed 8 September 2018).

Better Work 2015. "Working conditions, productivity and profitability: evidence from Better Work Vietnam". Geneva: ILO. Available at: https://betterwork.org/blog/portfolio/working-conditions-productivity-and-profitability-evidence-from-better-work-vietnam/ (accessed 8 September 2018).

Bettio, F. *et al.* 2013. "The impact of the economic crisis on the situation of women and men and on gender equality policies". Luxembourg: European Union.

Blackett, A. 2017. "Domestic workers and informality: compliance with decent work for domestic workers as a transgression to the asymmetrical law of the home workplace". WIEGO Twentieth Anniversary Research Conference.

Blackett, A. & C. Sheppard 2003. "Collective bargaining and equality: making connections". *International Labour Review* 142(4), 419–57.

Bleijenbergh, I., J. de Bruijn & L. Dickens 2001. "Strengthening and mainstreaming equal opportunities through collective bargaining". Dublin: European Foundation for the Improvement of Living and Working Conditions.

BNP Paribas–SNB/CFE-GCS 2014. Accord sure le harcèlement et la violence au travail. Paris: BNP Paribas & SNB/CFE-GCS.

Bonner, C., P. Horn & R. Jhabvala 2018. "Informal women workers open ILO Doors through transnational organizing 1980s–2010s". In E. Boris,

D.Hoehtker & S. Zimmermann (eds) *Women's ILO: Transnational Networks, Global Labour Standards and Gender Equity, 1919 to Present.* Geneva: ILO.

Bonner, C., StreetNet International & WIEGO 2009. "Recruiting informal workers into democratic workers' organisations". StreetNet International & WIEGO. Available at: http://wiego.org/sites/wiego.org/files/resources/files/ICC1-Recruiting-Informal-Workers-Orgs-English.pdf (accessed 8 September 2018).

Briskin, L. 2006. "Equity bargaining/bargaining equity". Working paper series: Restructuring Work and Labour in the New Economy, updated and revised. University of York. Available at: http://www.yorku.ca/lbriskin/pdf/bargainingpaperFINAL3secure.pdf (accessed 8 September 2018).

Briskin, L. 2014a. "Strategies to support equality bargaining inside unions: representational democracy and representational justice". *Journal of Industrial Relations* 56(2), 208–27.

Briskin, L. 2014b. "Austerity, union policy and gender equality bargaining". *Transfer* 20(1), 115–33.

Briskin, L. & A. Muller 2011. "Promoting gender equality through social dialogue: global trends and persistent obstacles". Industrial and Employment Relations Department working paper 34. Geneva: ILO.

Brown, D. *et al.* 2014. "Are sweatshops profit-maximizing? Answer: no. Evidence from Better Work Vietnam". Better Work discussion paper no.17.

Budlender, D. 2011. "Gender equality and social dialogue in South Africa". Working paper 2/2011. Geneva: ILO.

Bureau of Labor Statistics, Department of Labor 2013. "Pay and benefits: paid leave in private industry over the last 20 years by Robert W. Van Glezen". In *Beyond the Numbers* 2(18), 1–6.

BusinessEurope, ETUC, CEEP, UEAPME 2007. Implementation of the European Autonomous Framework Agreement on Harassment and Violence at Work. Brussels: BusinessEurope, ETUC, CEEP, UEAPME.

BusinessEurope, ETUC, CEEP, UEAPME 2011. Implementation of the European Autonomous Framework Agreement on Harassment and Violence at Work. Final joint report by the European Social Partners adopted at the Social Dialogue Committee on 27 October 2011.

BusinessEurope, UEAPME, CEEP and ETUC 2014. "A Toolkit for Gender Equality in Practice: 100 Initiatives by Social Partners and in the Workplace across Europe". Brussels: ETUC.

BWI 2017. "Case study: violence against brick kiln workers (India)". Cited in J. Pillinger (2017b) "Violence and harassment against women and men in the world of work". Geneva: ILO.

Cabrita, J. & F. Wohlgemuth 2015. "Promoting uptake of parental and paternity leave among fathers in the European Union". Dublin: Eurofound.

Carrefour-UNI 2015. International Agreement for the Promotion of Social Dialogue and Diversity and Respect for Basic Employee Rights.

Carrefour-UNI 2018. Accord International pour la promotion du dialogue social et de la diversité, et pour le respect des droits fondamentaux au travail (signed 3 October 2018).

CARVE 2016. "Responding to violence against women: guide for companies". Paris: CARVE. Available at: http://carve-daphne.eu/wp-content/resources/CARVEguideEN.PDF (accessed 8 September 2018).

CCOO 2014. "Guia sindical sobre violències masclistes a la feina (by S. Morreres, A. Garcia A & L. Sandalinas)". Secretaria de Politica Territorial i Barcelonès de CCOO de Catalunya. Available at: http://www.ccoo.cat/pdf_documents/2015/201501_guiaViolenciaMasclista_interior_web.pdf (accessed 8 September 2018).

CCOO 2016a. No A Les Violencies Masclistes, Volem ser LLiures. CCOO Informe 25 de Novembre de 2016. Elaboració Alba García, Lidia Sandalinas, Gina Argemir, Mar Meneses, Isabel Ortega. CCOO secretaria de la dona. Available at: http://www.ccoo.cat/pdf_documents/2016/informe_25N2016_CCOO.pdf (accessed 8 September 2018).

CCOO 2016b. Protocolo contra el acoso sexual y por razón de sexo y contra el acoso por razón de orientación sexual, identidad de género y/o expresión de género. Available at: http://www.fsc.ccoo.es/a0177faa67f3f71b5632579aeead3688000050.pdf (accessed 8 September 2018)

CEMR/EPSU 2007. "Guidelines to drawing up gender equality action plans in local and regional government". Brussels: CEMR/EPSU. Available at: http://www.epsu.org/a/3541 (accessed 8 September 2018).

Chant, S. & C. Pedwell 2008. "Women, gender and the informal economy: An assessment of ILO research and suggested ways forward". Geneva: ILO.

Cobble, D. 2012. "Gender equality and labor movements: toward a global perspective". Washington, DC: Solidarity Centre.

Cockburn, C. 1991. *In the Way of Women: Men's Resistance to Sex Equality in Organizations*. Basingstoke: Palgrave Macmillan.

Colgan, F. & S. Ledwith 1996. "Sisters organizing: women and their trade unions". In S. Ledwith *et al.* (eds) *Women in Organisations*. Basingstoke: Palgrave Macmillan.

Colgan, F. & S. Ledwith (eds) 2002. *Gender, Diversity and Trade Unions: International Perspectives*. New York: Routledge.

COSATU 2016. "Gender, politics and trade unions". Available at: http://www.cosatu.org.za/docs/policy/2016/Gender-Politics-and-Trade-Unions.pdf (accessed 8 September 2018).

Council of Europe 2011. "Explanatory Report to the Council of Europe Convention on preventing and combating violence against women and domestic violence". Strasbourg: Council of Europe. Available at: https://rm.coe.int/CoERMPublicCommonSearchServices/DisplayDCTMContent?documentId=09000016800d383a (accessed 8 September 2018).

Cruz, A. 2012. "Good practices and challenges on the Maternity Protection Convention, 2000 (no. 183) and the Workers with Family Responsibilities Convention 1981 (no. 156): A comparative study". Working Paper 2/12. Bureau for Gender Equality. Geneva: ILO.

Cruz, A. & S. Klinger 2011. "Gender-based violence in the world of work: overview and selected annotated bibliography". Geneva: ILO.

CUPE 2013. "Residential long-term care in Canada: our vision for better seniors' care". Available at: http://cupe.ca/sites/cupe/files/CUPE-long-term-care-seniors-care-vision.pdf (accessed 8 September 2018).

CUPE 2017. "It's time to care: Ontario seniors need a minimum 4 hour daily care standard to be the law". Available at: https://cupe.ca/its-time-care-ontario-seniors-need-minimum-4-hour-daily-care-standard-be-law (accessed 8 September 2018).

CUPE 2018. "Workplace violence and harassment prevention kit". Available at https://cupe.ca/cupes-workplace-violence-and-harassment-prevention-kit-available-online (accessed 8 September 2018).

CUPE Equality 2014. "Workplace harassment and mental injuries: examining root causes". Available at: http://cupe.ca/sites/cupe/files/harassment_and_mental_injuries.pdf (accessed 8 September 2018).

Dau-Schmidt, K. 2007. "The changing face of collective representation: the future of collective bargaining". *Chicago-Kent Law Review* 82, 903–30.

Dawson, T. 2014. "Collective bargaining and the gender pay gap in the printing industry". *Gender, Work and Organization* 21, 381–94.

Dawson, T. 2018. *Gender, Class and Power: An Analysis of Pay Inequalities in the Workplace*. London: Palgrave Macmillan.

De Henau, J., D. Perrons & S. Himmelweit 2017. "Investing in the care economy: simulating employment effects by gender in countries in emerging economies". Brussels: ITUC.

Deakin, S. *et al.* 2015. "Are litigation and collective bargaining complements or substitutes for achieving gender equality? A study of the British Equal Pay Act". *Cambridge Journal of Economics*, 39(2), 381–403.

Department for Business, Innovation and Skills 2015. Trade Union Membership 2015. *Statistical Bulletin.* London: DBIS. Available at: https://www.gov. uk/government/uploads/system/uploads/attachment_data/file/525938/ Trade_Union_Membership_2015_-_Statistical_Bulletin.pdf (accessed 8 September 2018).

Department for International Development (DFID)/International Development Research Centre (IDRC) 2012. "Women's economic empowerment and inclusive growth: labour markets and enterprise development". SIG working paper, 2012/1. Report by N. Kabeer. London: DFID/IDRC.

Dias, S. & A. Ogando 2015. "Rethinking gender and waste: exploratory findings from participatory action research in Brazil". *Work Organization, Labour & Globalization* 9(2), 51–63.

Dickens, L. 1998. "Illuminating the process: equal opportunities and collective bargaining in Europe". Dublin: European Foundation for the Improvement of Living and Working Conditions.

Dickens, L. 2000. "Collective bargaining and the promotion of gender equality at work: opportunities and challenges for trade unions". *Transfer* 6(2), 193–208.

Donald, K. & R. Moussié 2016. "Redistributing unpaid care work: why tax matters for women's rights". IDS policy briefing 109. Brighton: Institute for Development Studies.

Eade, D. 2004. "International NGOs and unions in the South: worlds apart or allies in the struggle?" *Development in Practice* 14(1/2), 71–84.

Eaton, A., S. Schurman & M. Chen (eds) 2017. *Informal Workers and Collective Action: A Global Perspective.* Ithaca, NY: Cornell University Press/ILR Press.

Education International (EI) 2012. "Final Report. Global Dialogue Forum on Conditions of Personnel in Early Childhood Education". Geneva.

Elson, D. & R. Pearson 2015. "Transcending the impact of the financial crisis in the United Kingdom: towards plan F – a feminist economic strategy". *Feminist Review* 109, 8–30.

Enel Group, IndustriAll and PSI 2013. Global Framework Agreement (Rome). Available at: http://www.epsu.org/sites/default/files/article/files/19-_Enel_ Global_Framework_Agreement_-_inglese_14_giu_2013.pdf (accessed 8 September 2018).

EPSU/European Social Dialogue Committee for Central Administration 2011. "Toward equal pay for women and men". Brussels: EPSU.

EPSU-HOSPEEM-CEMR-UNIEUROPA-EUROCOMMERCE- ETUCE-EFEE-CoESS 2013a. "Multi-sectoral guidelines to tackle third-party violence and harassment related to work". Brussels.

EPSU-HOSPEEM-CEMR-UNIEUROPA-EUROCOMMERCE- ETUCE-EFEE-CoESS 2013b. "Report on the follow-up and implementation of the multi-sectoral guidelines to tackle work-related third-party violence". Brussels.

EPSU-UNI 2009. "Policies, strategies and implementation: how issues of third-party violence have been tackled in practice by social partners in the commerce, hospital, private security and local and regional government sectors". Available at: http://www.epsu.org/sites/default/files/article/files/EN_UNI_EPSU_report-2.pdf (accessed 8 September 2018).

Espino, A. & G. Pedetti 2012. "Social dialogue and gender equality in Uruguay". Working paper no. 15. Geneva: ILO. Available at: http://www.ilo.org/wcmsp5/groups/public/---ed_dialogue/---dialogue/documents/publication/wcms_187872.pdf (accessed 8 September 2018).

ETUC, Business Europe, CEEP & UEAPME 2013. "Social partner involvement in European economic governance: declaration by the European social partners". Brussels.

ETUC, CEEP, UNICE & UEAPME 2005. "Framework of actions on gender equality". Brussels.

ETUCE-EFEE 2012. "Social partners in education concerned about violence in schools: 'how to prevent and mitigate third-party violence and harassment in schools'". Warsaw.

EU-OSHA 2011. "Workplace violence and harassment: a European picture". Luxembourg: European Union.

Eurofound 2010. "Addressing the gender pay gap: government and social partner actions". Report by A. Ponzellini, C. Aumayr & F. Wolf. Dublin: Eurofound.

Eurofound 2013a. "Women, men and working conditions in Europe". Luxembourg: European Union.

Eurofound 2013b. "Tackling undeclared work in 27 European Union member states and Norway: approaches and measures since 2008". Dublin: Eurofound.

Eurofound 2014a. "Social partners and gender equality in Europe". Luxembourg: European Union.

Eurofound 2014b. "Pay in Europe in the 21st century". Luxembourg: European Union.

Eurofound 2015a. "Violence and harassment in European workplaces: causes, impacts and policies". Dublin: Eurofound.

Eurofound 2015b. "Social partner organisations: the long march towards gender equality". Foundation Focus. Dublin: Eurofound.

Eurofound 2018. "Pay transparency in Europe: first experiences with gender pay reports and audits in four member states". Luxembourg: European Union.

Eurofound & EU-OSHA 2014. "Psychosocial risks in Europe: prevalence and strategies for prevention". Luxembourg: European Union.

European Commission 2012. "The role of men in gender equality". Prepared for the European Commission by a consortium led by L&R Social Research. Brussels: European Commission.

European Commission 2014. Commission Recommendation of 7.3.2014 on strengthening the principle of equal pay between men and women through transparency, C(2014) 1405 final.

European Commission 2016a. Proposal for a Council Decision on the signing, on behalf of the European Union, of the Council of Europe Convention on preventing and combating violence against women and domestic violence. COM(2016)111.

European Commission 2016b. Proposal for a Council Decision, on the conclusion, by the European Union, of the Council of Europe Convention on preventing and combating violence against women and domestic violence. COM(2016)109.

European Commission 2016c. "Closing the gender pay gap". Summary report of the EU Mutual Learning Seminar on Gender Equality. Brussels: European Commission.

European Commission 2017a. Proposal for a Directive of the European Parliament and of the Council on work-life balance for parents and carers and repealing Council Directive 2010/18/EU.

European Commission 2017b. "Report on the implementation of Commission Recommendation on strengthening the principle of equal pay between men and women through transparency" (COM(2017) 671 final). Luxembourg: European Union.

European Commission 2017c. "The impact of various tax systems on gender equality". EU Mutual Learning Programme in Gender Equality, Sweden. Brussels: European Commission.

European Commission Advisory Group on Equal Opportunities for Women and Men 2009. "Opinion on the gender perspective on the response to the economic and financial crisis". Brussels: European Commission, Employment, Social Affairs and Opportunities.

European Commission, European Council & European Parliament 2017. "European Pillar of Social Rights". Brussels: European Commission.

European Federation of Journalists (EFJ) undated. "A handbook on gender equality best practices in European journalists' unions". Brussels: EFJ/Friedrich Ebert Stiftung. Available at: http://www.ifj.org/fileadmin/images/Gender/ Gender_documents/Gender_Equality_Best_Practices_Handbook_-_ English_version.pdf (accessed 8 September 2018).

European Federation of Public Service Unions (EPSU) 2010. "EPSU gender mainstreaming audit". Brussels: EPSU.

European Federation of Public Service Unions (EPSU) 2011. "Reducing the gender pay gap – implementing the equal pay resolutions from the 2009 EPSU Congress Report 2010". Brussels: EPSU.

European Federation of Public Service Unions (EPSU) 2013. "The gender pay gap in public services". Brussels: EPSU.

European Federation of Public Service Unions (EPSU) 2018. "Towards a new gender contract: implementing gender equality in times of crisis". Conference briefing, Prague. Brussels: EPSU.

European Institute for Gender Equality (EIGE) 2014. "Estimating the costs of gender-based violence in the European Union: report". Luxembourg: European Union. Available at: http://eige.europa.eu/rdc/eige-publications/estimating-costs-gender-based-violence-european-union-report (accessed 8 September 2018).

European Parliament 2009. "Women and unpaid family care work in the EU". Brussels: European Parliament.

European Parliament 2013. "European added value assessment: application of the principle of equal pay for men and women for equal work of equal value". An assessment accompanying the European Parliament's Legislative own-Initiative Report (Rapporteur Edit Bauer, MEP). Brussels: European Parliament.

European Trade Union Committee for Education (ETUCE) 2010. "Updated ETUCE action plan on preventing and tackling violence in schools". Adopted by the ETUCE Executive Board in Brussels on 23 November 2010. Brussels: ETUCE.

European Trade Union Confederation (ETUC) 2006. "Challenging times: innovative ways of organising working time". Brussels: ETUC.

European Trade Union Confederation (ETUC) 2010. "From membership to leadership: advancing the position of women in trade unions". Report by J. Pillinger for the ETUC women's committee. Brussels: ETUC. Available at: http://www.etuc.org/publications/membership-leadership-advancing-women-trade-unions-resource-guide#.U0F4YVx6cll (accessed 8 September 2018).

European Trade Union Confederation (ETUC) 2011a. "Strategy and action programme 2011–2015". Adopted at the ETUC 12th Statutory Congress, Athens. Brussels: ETUC.

European Trade Union Confederation (ETUC) 2011b. "Working for better times: working time regulation and innovation in the 21st century". Report by J. Pillinger. Brussels: ETUC. Available at: https://www.etuc.org/sites/default/files/CES_tempsMeilleurs_Uk_1.pdf (accessed 8 September 2018).

European Trade Union Confederation (ETUC) 2012. "Solidarity in the crisis and beyond: a social contract for Europe". ETUC resolution adopted by the executive committee on 5–6 June 2012. Brussels: ETUC.

European Trade Union Confederation (ETUC) 2013a. Final Statement adopted by the Collective Bargaining Coordination Committee in the ETUC Collective Bargaining School, Florence.

European Trade Union Confederation (ETUC) 2013b. The ETUC Coordination of Collective Bargaining and Wages in the EU Economic Governance. ETUC Executive Committee. Brussels: ETUC.

European Trade Union Confederation (ETUC) 2016. ETUC position on the second stage consultation of the social partners at European level under Article 154 TFEU on possible action addressing the challenges of work-life balance faced by working parents and caregivers. Brussels: ETUC.

European Trade Union Confederation (ETUC) 2017a. ETUC assessment of the EU Commission Package on work-life balance. Brussels: ETUC

European Trade Union Confederation (ETUC) 2017b. Annual General Equality survey 2017. Brussels: ETUC

European Trade Union Confederation (ETUC) 2018. "Baden-Württemberg metal workers' pay rise and work time flexibility sets German precedent and EU example". Brussels: ETUC. Available at https://www.etuc.org/press/baden-wurttemburg-metal-workers-pay-rise-and-work-time-flexibility-sets-german-precedent-eu#.WpTFj1cVvFQ (accessed 8 September 2018).

European Trade Union Institute (ETUI) 2018. "IG Metall wins right to a 28-hour week and wage deal". *ETUI Collective Bargaining Newsletter* 2. Brussels: ETUI.

European Transport Federation 2017. "Violence against women transport workers: Summary report". Brussels: ETF.

Evans, A. 2017. "The politics of better work for women: Vietnam's garment industry. Gender and politics in practice". University of Birmingham and La Trobe University.

Evers, B., F. Amoding & A. Krishnan 2014. "Social and economic upgrading in floriculture global value chains: flowers and cuttings GVCs in Uganda". Capturing the Gains working paper 2014/42. University of Manchester.

Fagan, C., A. Hegewisch & J. Pillinger 2006. "Out of time: why Britain needs a new approach to working time flexibility". University of Manchester/TUC.

Fagan, C. & J. Rubery 2018. "Advancing gender equality through European employment policy: the impact of the UK's EU membership and the risks of Brexit". *Social Policy and Society* 17(2), 297–317.

Fair Wear Foundation (FWF) 2018a. "Breaking the silence: Fair Wear Foundation violence and harassment prevention programme". Amsterdam: FWF.

Fair Wear Foundation (FWF) 2018b. "Violence against women and men in the global garment supply chain". FWF contribution to the standard-setting discussions at the 107th Internaitonal Labour Conference on ending violence and harassment against women and men in the world of work. Amsterdam: FWF.

Fuchs, G. 2010. "Promising paths to pay equity: a comparison of the potentials of strategic litigation, collective bargaining and anti-discrimination authorities in Switzerland, Germany and France". Social Science Research Network.

GDF-Suez Group 2012. "European agreement on professional equality between women and men". Paris/Brussels: GDF-Suez/EPSU.

Goldsmith, M. 2013. "Collective bargaining and domestic workers in Uruguay case study". Manchester/Cambridge, MA: WIEGO.

Green, D. 2008. "Reducir la brecha salarial de género. Aplicando sistemas de evaluación de puestos para revalorizar el trabajo tradicional de mujeres. Una guía práctica para las organizaciones sindicales y gremiales del sector público". Ferney-Voltaire: PSI. Available at: http://www.world-psi.org/sites/default/files/documents/research/sp_reduciendo_la_brecha_salarial.pdf (accessed 8 September 2018).

Gregory, A. & S. Milner 2009. "Trade unions and work-life balance: changing times in France and the UK?" *British Journal of Industrial Relations* 47(1), 122–46.

Grimshaw, D., G. Bosch & J. Rubery 2014. "Minimum wages and collective bargaining: what types of pay bargaining can foster positive pay equity outcomes?". *British Journal of Industrial Relations* 52(3), 470–98.

Grimshaw, D., J. Rubery & S. Marino 2012. "Public sector pay and procurement in Europe during the crisis". EWERC working paper. Manchester Business School.

Grünell, M. 2006. "Mainstreaming gender at the social partner table in Europe". *Transfer* 12(1), 49–60.

Grünell, M. & M. Schaapman 2005. "Gender mainstreaming in industrial relations". In European Industrial Relations Observatory On-line (EIRO).

Guillaume, C. 2013. "La mobilisation des syndicats anglais en faveur de l'égalité salariale (1968-2012)". *Travail, Genre et Sociétés* 30, 93–110.

H&M, IndustriALL, IF Metall 2015. "Global Framework Agreement between H&M Hennes & Mauritz GBC AB and IndustriALL Global Union and Industrifacket Metall on Compliance and implementation of International Labour Standards at the Suppliers of H&M Hennes & Mauritz GBC AB".

Available at: http://www.industriall-union.org/sites/default/files/uploads/documents/GFAs/HM/hm_gfa2016_eng.pdf (accessed 8 September 2018).

Hadwiger, F. 2015a. "Global framework agreements: achieving decent work in global supply chains?" *International Journal of Labour Research* 7(1/2), 75–94.

Hadwiger, F. 2015b. "Global framework agreements: achieving decent work in global supply chains". Background paper. Geneva: ILO.

Hansen, L. 2004. "Does the future of unions depend on the integraton of diversity?" *Industrielle Beziehungen* 11, 129–42.

Hayter, S. 2015. "Unions and collective bargaining". In B. Janine (ed.) *Labour Markets, Institutions and Inequality*. Geneva: ILO.

Hayter, S. & B. Weinberg 2011. "Mind the gap: collective bargaining and wage inequality". In S. Hayter (ed.) *The Role of Collective Bargaining in the Global Economy: Negotiating for Social Justice*. Geneva: ILO.

Heeks, R. 2017. "Decent work and the digital gig economy: a developing country perspective on employment impacts and standards in online outsourcing, crowdwork, etc.". Geneva: ILO.

Heery, E. 2006. "Equality bargaining: where, who, why?" *Gender, Work & Organization* 13, 522–42.

Hobden, C. 2015. "Domestic workers organize – but can they bargain? Mapping collective bargaining and other forms of negotiation in the domestic work sector". ILO's Work in Progress. Geneva: ILO. Available at: http://www.ilo.org/wcmsp5/groups/public/---ed_protect/---protrav/---travail/documents/publication/wcms_345704.pdf (accessed 8 September 2018).

HRCT (Nordic Union) 2016. "Hotels, restaurants, catering and tourism: overview of research on sexual harassment in the Nordic hotel, restaurant and tourism industry". Copenhagen: HRCT.

Human Rights Watch 2012. "Cultivating fear: the vulnerability of immigrant farmworkers in the US to sexual violence and sexual harassment". New York: Human Rights Watch.

Inditex and IndustriALL 2014. Global framework agreement between INDITEX S.A. and IndustriALL Global Union on the implementation of international labour standards throughout the suppy chain of Inditex. Available at: http://www.industriall-union.org/sites/default/files/uploads/documents/GFAs/signed_gfa_inditex_-_english.pdf (accessed 8 September 2018).

International Commission of Jurists (ICJ) 2016. Proposals for Elements of a Legally Binding Instrument on Transnational Corporations and Other Business Enterprises. Geneva. Available at https://www.icj.org/wp-content/uploads/2016/10/Universal-OEWG-session-2-ICJ-submission-Advocacy-Analysis-brief-2016-ENG.pdf (accessed 8 September 2018).

International Labour Organization (ILO) 2002. "Promoting gender equality through collective bargaining: a resource kit for unions". Geneva: ILO.

International Labour Organization (ILO) 2007. "Global financial agreements: a global tool for supporting rights at work". Geneva: ILO.

International Labour Organization (ILO) 2009a. "Resolution concerning gender equality at the heart of decent work". International Labour Conference, 98th Session, Geneva. Geneva: ILO.

International Labour Organization (ILO) 2009b. "Report of the Committee of Experts on the application of conventions and recommendations. Report III (Part 1A). General report and observations concerning particular countries". Geneva: ILO.

International Labour Organization (ILO) 2011. "Equality at work: the continuing challenge". Global report under the follow-up to the ILO Declaration on Fundamental Principles and Rights at Work. Geneva: ILO.

International Labour Organization (ILO) 2013a. "Social dialogue: recurrent discussion under the ILO Declaration on Social Justice for a Fair Globalization". International Labour Conference, report VI, 102nd session. Geneva: ILO.

International Labour Organization (ILO) 2013b "The informal economy and decent work: a policy resource guide, supporting transitions to formality". Geneva: ILO.

International Labour Organization (ILO) 2014a. "General survey on minimum wage systems". Geneva: ILO.

International Labour Organization (ILO) 2014b. "Transitioning from the informal to the formal economy". International Labour Conference, report V(1), 103rd session. Geneva: ILO.

International Labour Organization (ILO) 2015a. "Domestic workers organize – but can they bargain?" ILO's Work in Progress. Geneva: ILO.

International Labour Organization (ILO) 2015b. "World employment and social outlook: trends 2015". Geneva: ILO.

International Labour Organization (ILO) 2016a. "Decent work in global supply chains". International Labour Conference, report IV, 105th session. Geneva: ILO.

International Labour Organization (ILO) 2016a. "Global wage report 2016/17: wage inequality in the workplace". Geneva: ILO.

International Labour Organization (ILO) 2016b. "Non-standard employment around the world". Geneva: ILO.

International Labour Organization (ILO) 2016c. "Closing the gender pay gap: a review of the issues, policy mechanisms and international evidence". Geneva: ILO.

International Labour Organization (ILO) 2016d. Report of the Director-General, Fifth Supplementary Report: Outcome of the Meeting of Experts on Violence against Women and Men in the World of Work. ILO Governing Body, 328th Session, Geneva, 27 October–10 November. Geneva: ILO.

International Labour Organization (ILO) 2016e. Background paper for discussion at the Meeting of Experts on Violence against Women and Men in the World of Work, 3–6 October. Geneva: ILO.

International Labour Organization (ILO) 2017a. Inception Report for the Global Commission on the Future of Work. Geneva: ILO.

International Labour Organization (ILO) 2017b. "World employment and social outlook: trends for women 2017". Geneva: ILO.

International Labour Organization (ILO) 2018a. "Ending violence and harassment in the world of work". Report V (2) ("Yellow Report"). Geneva: ILO.

International Labour Organization (ILO) 2018b. Reports of the Standard-Setting Committee: Resolution and proposed Conclusions submitted for adoption by the Conference. 107th Session, Geneva, May–June. Geneva: ILO.

International Labour Organization (ILO) 2018c. "Addressing care for inclusive labour markets and gender equality". Issue Brief #3. Prepared for the 2nd Meeting of the Global Commission on the Future of Work, 15–17 February 2018. Geneva: ILO.

International Labour Organization (ILO) 2018d. "Women and men in the informal economy: a statistical picture". Third edition. Geneva: ILO.

International Labour Organization (ILO) 2018e. "International framework agreements in the food retail, garment and chemicals sectors: lessons learned from three case studies". Geneva: ILO.

International Labour Organization (ILO) 2018f. "Employment terms and conditions in tertiary education". Issues paper for discussion at the Global Dialogue Forum on Employment Terms and Conditions in Tertiary Education, Geneva, 18-20 September. Geneva: ILO.

International Labour Organization (ILO) 2018g. Resolution concerning the second recurrent discussion on social dialogue and tripartism, adopted by the ILC, 7 June 2018. Geneva, ILO.

International Labour Organization (ILO), UN Women & OECD 2017. "ILO, UN Women and OECD's vision for the equal pay international coalition (EPIC)". Geneva: ILO.

International Trade Union Confederation (ITUC) undated. "Stop gender-based violence at work". campaign newsletter. Available at: https://www.ituc-csi. org/gbv-campaign-newsletter-1 (accessed 8 September 2018).

International Trade Union Confederation (ITUC) 2009. "The decent work agenda: a gender perspective". Brussels: ITUC. Available at: http://www. ituc-csi.org/IMG/pdf/women_report_EN.pdf (accessed 8 September 2018).

International Trade Union Confederation (ITUC) 2011a. "Living with economic insecurity: women in precarious work". Brussels: ITUC.

International Trade Union Confederation (ITUC) 2011b. "Decisions for life: empowering young women to lead". Brussels: ITUC.

International Trade Union Confederation (ITUC) 2016. "Campaign toolkit: stop gender-based violence at work – support an ILO Convention". Available at: https://www.ituc-csi.org/campaign-toolkit-stop-gender-based (accessed 8 September 2018).

International Trade Union Confederation (ITUC) 2017. "ITUC global rights index: the world's worst countries for workers". Brussels: ITUC.

International Transport Federation (ITF) undated. "Action guide on violence against women". London: ITF.

International Transport Federation (ITF) 2016. "Informal transport workers' charter". London: ITF.

International Transport Federation (ITF) 2017. "Case study: women informal transport workers (Uganda)". Cited in J. Pillinger (2017b) "Violence and harrassment against women and men in the world of work". Geneva: ILO.

International Union of Food, Agricultural, Hotel, Restaurant, Catering, Tobacco and Allied Workers' Associations (IUF) undated. "Zero tolerance for sexual harassment at Sodexo". Available at: http://www.iuf.org/w/sites/default/files/ SODEXOsexualharassementA5bookletagreementPRINTe.pdf (accessed 8 September 2018).

International Union of Food, Agricultural, Hotel, Restaurant, Catering, Tobacco and Allied Workers' Associations (IUF) 2007. "All for one and one for all: a gender equality guide for trade unionists in the agriculture, food, hotel and catering sectors". Geneva: IUF.

International Union of Food, Agricultural, Hotel, Restaurant, Catering, Tobacco and Allied Workers' Associations (IUF) 2017. Resolutions adopted by the 27th Congress. Resolution No 18 Menstruation – a workplace and trade union issue. IUF Congress, Geneva, 29 August–1 September 2017. Available at: http://www.iuf.org/27thcongress/wp-content/uploads/2017/06/ Resolutions-adopted-by-the-27th-Congress.pdf) (accessed 8 September 2018).

IUF-IndustriaALL-UNILEVER 2016. Joint commitment to prevent sexual harassment. Available at: http://www.industriall-union.org/sites/default/ files/uploads/documents/2016/iuf-_industriall-unilever_joint_ commitment_to_preventing_sexual_harassment.pdf (accessed 8 September 2018).

Jayasinghe, D. 2014. "Unpaid care and public services". Presentation to PSI World Women's Committee, 23 June. Ferney-Voltaire: PSI.

Jepsen, M. & J. Leschke 2011. "The economic crisis – challenge or opportunity for gender equality in social policy outcomes? A comparison of Denmark, Germany and the UK". European Trade Union Institute working paper. Brussels: ETUI.

Johnston, H. & C. Land-Kazlauskas 2018. "Organizing on-demand: representation, voice, and collective bargaining in the gig economy". Conditions of Work and Employment Series No. 94. Geneva: ILO.

Kaminski, M. & E. Yakura 2008. "Women's union leadership: closing the gender gap". *WorkingUSA: The Journal of Labor and Society* 11, 459–75.

Kapoor, A. 2007. "The SEWA way: shaping another future for informal labour" In *Futures* 39(5), 554–68.

Karamessini, M. & J. Rubery 2014. *Women and Austerity: The Economic Crisis and the Future of Gender Equality.* Abingdon: Routledge.

Keifman, S., & R. Maurizio 2012. "Changes in labour market conditions and policies: their impact on wage inequality during the last decade". UNU-WIDER Working Paper 2012/14. Helsinki.

Kirsch, A. & S. Blaschke 2014. "Women's quotas and their effects: a comparison of Austrian and German trade unions". *European Journal of Industrial Relations* 20(3), 201–17.

Kirton, G. 2000. "Women, power and trade union government in the UK". *British Journal of Industrial Relations* 38: 343–60.

Knüttel, A. 2013. "Bargaining for work life balance: vereinbarkeit von arbeit und leben gestalten!". IG Metall Vorstand. Presentation to the ETUC Bargaining for Equality conference, Vilnius, 5–6 November 2014.

Ledwith, S. 2012. "Gender politics in trade unions: the representation of women between exclusion and inclusion". *Transfer* 18(2), 185–99.

Ledwith, S. & J. Munakamwe 2015. "Gender, union leadership and collective bargaining: Brazil and South Africa". *Economic and Labour Relations Review* 26(3), 411–29.

Leonardi, S. & B. De Sario 2012. "Contrattazione collet- tiva, pari opportunità e conciliazione: una panoramica nazionale e aziendale. Ricerca per il convegno della CGIL "Le donne cambiano....la contrattazione". Rome: GGIL.

Local Government Denmark, Danish Regions & KTO (Danish Association of Local Government Employees' Organisations) 2010. "Harassment and violence in Danish municipal and regional workplaces". Available at: http://

www.kl.dk/ImageVaultFiles/id_46479/cf_202/Avoiding_Harassment_and_
Violence.PDF (accessed 8 September 2018).

Lopes, C. & S. Mapker (eds) 2016. *Challenging Partriarchy: Conversations on Violence Against Women*. Cape Town: Heinrich Böll Stiftung.

MacGregor, J., C. Wathen & B. MacQuarrie 2016. "Domestic violence in the Canadian workplace: are co-workers aware?". *Safety and Health at Work* 7(3), 244–50.

Maier, F. 2010. "Re-cession or He-cession? Gender dimensions of economic crisis and economic policy". In A. Watt & A. Botsch (eds), *After the Crisis: Towards A Sustainable Growth Model*. Brussels: ETUI.

Martinez-Vazquez, J., B. Moreno-Dodson & V. Vulovic 2012. "The impact of tax and expenditure policies on income distribution: evidence from a large panel of countries". International Center for Public Policy working paper 12/25. Available at: https://scholarworks.gsu.edu/icepp/77/ (accessed 8 September 2018).

McBride, J. & I. Greenwood 2009. *Community Unionism: A Comparative Analysis of Concepts and Contexts*. Basingstoke: Palgrave Macmillan.

McFerran, L. 2011. "Safe at home, safe at work? National domestic violence and the workplace survey". Sydney: Australian Domestic and Family Violence Clearinghouse.

McFerran, L. 2016. "Domestic violence is a workplace issue: Australian developments 2009–2016". Available at: https://www.wgea.gov.au/sites/default/files/mcferran-domestic-violence-workplace-issue-australian-developments.pdf (accessed 8 September 2018).

Milner, S. & A. Gregory 2014. "Gender equality bargaining in France and the UK: an uphill struggle?" *Journal of Industrial Relations* 56(2), 246–63.

Mishel, M. & L. Walters 2003. "How unions help all workers". Washington, DC: Economic Policy Institute. Available at: https://www.epi.org/publication/briefingpapers_bp143/ (accessed 8 September 2018).

Moore, P. 2018. "The threat of physical and psychosocial violence and harassment in digitalized work". Geneva: ILO.

Morris, J. & J. Pillinger 2006. "Developing positive flexibility for employees: the British approach". In D. Perrons *et al.* (eds) *Gender Divisions and Working Time in the New Economy: Public Policy and Changing Patterns of Work in Europe and North America*. Cheltenham: Elgar.

Morris, J. & J. Pillinger 2016. "Gender-based violence in global supply chains: resource kit". Available at: http://www.itcilo.org/en/community/news/resource-kit-gender-based-violence-in-global-supply-chains (accessed 8 September 2018).

NASVI 2014. Street Vendors (Protection of Livelihood and Regulation of Street Vending) Act 2014. Available at: http://nasvinet.org/newsite/street-vendors-policies/ (accessed 8 September 2018).

National Mediation Office (Sweden) 2008. "Collective Bargaining and Wage Formation". Stockholm: National Mediation Office.

National Mediation Office (Sweden) 2014. "Wage differentials between men and women in 2014: what do the official statistics say?" Available at: http://www.mi.se/files/PDF-er/ar_foreign/eng_wage_differntials_2014.pdf (accessed 8 September 2018).

National Retail Association (NRA) 2016. "Family violence and the Australian retail industry: industry report". Available at: http://www.nra.net.au/wp-content/uploads/2015/09/RetailFV_Mar2016_Final.pdf (accessed 8 September 2018).

National Women's Law Centre (US) 2013. "Gender wage gap for union members is half the size of non-union workers' wage gap". Available at: https://nwlc.org/blog/gender-wage-gap-union-members-half-size-non-union-workers-wage-gap/ (accessed 8 September 2018).

Oelz, M. & U. Rani 2015. "Domestic work, wages, and gender equality: lessons from developing countries". Working Paper No. 5. ILO Gender, Equality and Diversity Branch. Geneva: ILO.

Oelz, M., S. Olney & M. Tomei 2013. "Equal pay: an introductory guide". International Labour Standards Department, Conditions of Work and Equality Department. Geneva: ILO.

Okechukwu, C. *et al.* 2014. "Discrimination, harassment, abuse, and bullying in the workplace: contribution of workplace injustice to occupational health disparities". *American Journal of Industrial Medicine* 57(5), 573–86.

Olsen, W. *et al.* 2010. "The gender wage gap in the UK 1995–2007: Part 2". University of Manchester: Cathy Marsh Centre for Census and Survey Research. London: Government Equalities Office.

Organisation for Economic Cooperation and Development (OECD) 2008. "The impact of foreign direct investment on wages and working conditions". Background paper to the OECD-ILO Conference on Corporate Social Responsibility, 23-24 June 2008. Paris: OECD.

Organisation for Economic Cooperation and Development (OECD) 2015. "FOCUS on minimum wages after the crisis: making them pay". Paris: OECD. Available at: http://www.oecd.org/social/Focus-on-Minimum-Wages-after-the-crisis-2015.pdf (accessed 8 September 2018).

Organisation for Economic Cooperation and Development (OECD) 2018. "OECD-ILO global deal for decent work and inclusive growth". Paris: OECD.

Otobe, N. 2017. "Gender and the informal economy: key challenges and policy response". Employment Department working paper No. 236. Geneva: ILO.

Oxfam International 2004. "Trading away our rights: women working in global supply chains". Oxford: Oxfam. Available at: https://www.oxfam.org/sites/www.oxfam.org/files/rights.pdf (accessed 8 September 2018).

Oxfam International 2018. "Reward work not wealth". Oxford: Oxfam. Available at: https://www.oxfam.org/sites/www.oxfam.org/files/file_attachments/bp-reward-work-not-wealth-220118-summ-en.pdf (accessed 8 September 2018).

Pardon, D. & P. Biard 2013. "Evaluation et classification des fonctions: un outil pour l'égalité". Presentation to the ETUC Bargaining for Equality conference, Vilnius, 5–6 November 2014.

Parker, J. & J. Douglas 2010. "The role of women's groups in NZ, UK and Canadian trade unions in addressing intersectional interests". *International Journal of Comparative Labour Law and Industrial Relations* 26(3), 295–320.

Parker, J. & J. Foley 2010. "Progress on women's equality within UK and Canadian trade unions: do women's structures make a difference?". *Relations Industrielles* 65(2), 281–303.

Parker, J. *et al.* 2011. "Comparative study on social dialogue and gender equality in New Zealand, Australia and Fiji". Geneva: ILO.

Perrons, D. & A. Plomien 2014. "Gender, inequality and the crisis: towards more equitable development". In M. Karamessini & J. Rubery (eds) *Women and Austerity: The Economic Crisis and the Future of Gender Equality*. New York, Routledge

Pillinger, J. 2014. "Bargaining for equality: how collective bargaining contributes to eliminating pay discrimination between women and men performing the same job or job of equal value". Brussels: ETUC.

Pillinger, J. 2017a. "Safe at home, safe at work: trade union strategies to prevent, manage and eliminate work-place harassment and violence against women". Brussels: ETUC.

Pillinger, J. 2017b. "Violence against women and men in the world of work: trade union perspectives and action". Geneva: ILO. Available at: http://www.ilo.org/actrav/info/pubs/WCMS_546645/lang--en/index.htm (accessed 8 September 2018).

Pillinger, J., V. Schmidt & N. Wintour 2016. "Negotiating for gender equality". Issue Brief No. 4, Labour relations and collective bargaining. Geneva: ILO.

Plantenga, J. & C. Remery 2006. "The gender pay gap: origins and policy responses. A comparative review of thirty European countries". Brussels: European Commission.

Ponzellini, A., C. Aumayr & F. Wolf 2010. "Addressing the gender pay gap: government and social partner actions". Dublin: European Foundation for the Improvement of Living and Working Conditions.

Prentice, R. *et al.* 2018. "Health and safety in garment workers' lives: setting a new research agenda". *Geoforum* 88, 157–60.

Preston, J. & C. Leffer 2016. "When 'best' is far from good enough: violations of workers' rights at four of H&M best-in-class suppliers in Cambodia". Oslo: Framtiden i våre hender.

PSI, ILO, ICN & WHO 2002. Framework guidelines for addressing workplace violence in the health sector. Geneva: PSI, ILO, ICN & WHO.

Public Services International (PSI) 2014. PSI statement: International Women's Day 2014. Available at: http://www.world-psi.org/en/psi-statemen t-international-womens-day-2014 (accessed 8 September 2018).

Public Services International (PSI) 2017. "People over profit: our time to lead. Programme of action 2018—2022". Adopted at the 30th PSI World Congress.

Public Services International (PSI) 2018. "Tackling violence in the health sector: a trade union response". Ferney Voltaire: PSI. Available at: http://www. who.int/violence_injury_prevention/violence/workplace/en/ (accessed 8 September 2018).

Public Services International (PSI) & Education International (EI) 2017. LGBT Forum. 30 October 2017, Geneva. Available at: http://congress.world-psi. org/wp-content/uploads/2017/09/EN_-LGBTForum_DraftProgramme.pdf (accessed 8 September 2018).

Rees, T. 1998. *Mainstreaming Equality in the European Union: Education, Training and Labour Market Policies*. London: Routledge.

Reeves, C. & A. O'Leary-Kelly 2009. "Study of the effects of intimate partner violence on the workplace". Washington, DC: US Department of Justice.

Resolution Foundation 2015. "Three in ten female workers set to benefit from new 'national living wage'". Press release. Available at: https://www. resolutionfoundation.org/media/press-releases/three-in-ten-female-workers-set-to-benefit-from-new-national-living-wage/ (accessed 8 September 2018).

Rosenbaum, J. & S. Silliman 2018. "Big brands: the missing voice in the fight to end gender-based violence at work". Open Democracy. Available at: https://www. opendemocracy.net/beyondslavery/jennifer-rosenbaum-shikha-silliman-bhattacharjee/big-brands-missing-voice-in-fight-to- (accessed 8 September 2018).

Rubery, J. & D. Grimshaw 2011. "Gender and the minimum wage". In S. Lee & D. McCann (eds) *Regulating for Decent Work*. Geneva: ILO.

Rubery, J. & D. Grimshaw 2015. "The 40-year pursuit of equal pay: a case of constantly moving goalposts". *Cambridge Journal of Economics* 39(2), 319–43.

Rubery, J. & R. Koukiadaki 2016. "Closing the gender pay gap: a review of the issues, policy mechanisms and international evidence". Gender and Diversity Branch. Geneva: ILO.

Sankaran, K. & R. Madhav 2011. "Gender equality and social dialogue in India". Geneva: ILO.

Schäfer, S. & S. Gottschall 2015. "From wage regulation to wage gap: how wage-setting institutions and structures shape the gender wage gap across three industries in 24 European countries and Germany". *Cambridge Journal of Economics* 39(2), 467–96.

Sechi, C. 2007. "Women in trade unions in Europe: bridging the gaps". Brussels: ETUC. Available at: http://www.etuc.org/IMG/pdf_English_complet.pdf (accessed 8 September 2018).

SEWA 2006. SEWA Joins the ICFTU July 2006. Available at http://www.sewa.org/july_2006.asp (accessed 8 September 2018).

SODEXO-IUF 2018. SODEXO-IUF Joint Commitment on preventing sexual harassment. Annex to the SODEXO-IUF international framework agreement of 12 December 2011. Available at: http://www.iuf.org/w/sites/default/files/JointCommitmentSODEXOIUFe.pdf (accessed 8 September 2018).

Standing, G. 2011. *The Precariat: The New Dangerous Class.* London: Bloomsbury Academic.

Standing, G. 2014. *A Precariat Charter: From Denizens to Citizens.* London: Bloomsbury Academic.

Staritz, C. & J. Guilherme Reis (eds) 2013. "Global value chains, economic upgrading, and gender: case studies of the horticulture, tourism, and call center industries". World Bank International Trade Department Gender Development Unit. Available at: http://www.capturingthegains.org/pdf/GVC_Gender_Report_web.pdf (accessed 8 September 2018).

Statistics Canada 2014. Union rates falling. Available online at: https://www150.statcan.gc.ca/n1/pub/11-630-x/11-630-x2015005-eng.htm (accessed 8 September 2018).

Stevis, D. 2010. "International framework agreements and global social dialogue: parameters and prospects". Geneva: ILO.

StreetNet International 2012. Summary report: case studies of collective bargaining and representative forums for street traders.

Stumbitz, B. *et al.* 2017. "Maternity protection and workers with family responsibilities in the formal and informal economy of Ghana: practices, gaps and measures for improvement". ILO working paper No. 3. Geneva: ILO.

Tilly, C. 2011. "Why austerity must not mean the end of active labour market policies". In Policy Network, *Priorities for a new Political Economy: Memos to the Left*. Available at: http://www.policy-network.net/publications/4002/priorities-for-a-new-political-economy-memos-to-the-left (accessed 4 October 2018).

TUC 2002. "Domestic violence: a guide for the workplace". London: TUC. Available at: https://www.tuc.org.uk/publications/domestic-violence-guide-workplace (accessed 8 September 2018).

TUC 2012. "Equality Audit Report 2012". London: TUC.

TUC 2014a. "Domestic violence and the workplace: a TUC survey report". London: TUC. Available at: https://www.tuc.org.uk/sites/default/files/Domestic_Violence_And_The_Workplace_0.pdf (accessed 8 September 2018).

TUC 2014b. "Equality Audit Report 2014". London: TUC.

TUC 2016. "Equality Audit Report 2016". London: TUC.

TUC 2017. "The rise of the 'gig' economy: workers at risk of missing out on key protections up 84% since 2006". Available at: https://www.tuc.org.uk/news/rise-"gig"-economy-workers-risk-missing-out-key-protections-84-2006 (accessed 8 September 2018).

TUCA 2016. Third Congress Documents and Resolutions, 26–29 April, São Paulo.

Tzannatos, Z. & A. Zabalza 1985. *Women and Equal Pay: The Effects of Legislation on Female Employment and Wages in Britain*. Cambridge: Cambridge University Press.

US Bureau of Labor Statistics 2016. Fatal occupational injuries in 2014: chart package. Available at: https://www.bls.gov/iif/oshwc/cfoi/cfch0013.pdf (accessed 8 September 2018).

United Nations 2013. Report on the fifty-seventh session of the Commission on the Status of Women, 4–15 March. New York: United Nations.

UNDP 2015. "Organizing informal workers: benefits, challenges and successes". Background paper for 2015 UNDP Human Development Report Office. New York: UNDP

UNESCO 2017. "School violence and bullying global status report". Paris: UNESCO.

UN General Assembly 2013. Report of the Special Rapporteur on extreme poverty and human rights. Geneva: UN General Assembly.

UN General Assembly 2016. Report of the Special Rapporteur on the rights to freedom of peaceful assembly and of association. Geneva: UN General Assembly.

UN Women 2015. "Progress of the world's women, 2015–16: transforming economies, realizing rights". New York: UN Women.

UN Women 2017. "Turning promises into action: gender equality in the 2030 agenda". Summary report. New York: UN Women.

UNISON 1999. "Raise the roof on domestic abuse: a UNISON guide to campaigning against domestic violence". London: UNISON.

UNISON 2015. "Domestic violence and abuse: a trade union issue. A UNISON guide". London: UNISON.

Vandekerckhove, S. 2013. "Bargaining in favour of low wage earners: different perspectives". Presentation to the ETUC 'Bargaining for Equality' conference, Vilnius, 5–6 November 2014.

Veldmann, A. 2017. "Pay transparency in the EU: A legal analysis of the situation in the EU Member States, Iceland, Liechtenstein and Norway". European network of legal experts in gender equality and non-discrimination, report for European Commission. Brussels: Directorate-General for Justice and Consumers.

Visser, J., S. Hayter & R. Gammarano 2015. "Trends in collective bargaining coverage: stability, erosion or decline?" Labour Relations and Collective Bargaining, issue brief no. 1. Geneva: ILO.

Walby, S. 2008. "The cost of domestic biolence: update 2009". Lancaster University.

Wathen, C., J. MacGregor, B. MacQuarrie, with the Canadian Labour Congress 2014. "Can work be safe, when home isn't? Initial findings of a pan-Canadian survey on domestic violence and the workplace". London, ON: Centre for Research & Education on Violence Against Women and Children.

World Health Organization (WHO) 2017. "Violence against women: intimate partner and sexual violence against women". Fact sheet. Geneva: WHO. Available at: http://www.who.int/mediacentre/factsheets/fs239/en/ (accessed 8 September 2018).

WIEGO 2015. "Delhi declaration of home-based workers". Available at: http://www.wiego.org/home-based-workers/delhi-declaration-of-home-e-based-workers (accessed 8 September 2018).

Williams, F. 2016. "Critical thinking in social policy: the challenges of past, present and future". *Social Policy & Administration* 50: 628–47.

Williamson, S. 2009. "Bargaining for gender equality in the Australian public service". *Labour & Industry* 20(2), 159–80.

Williamson, S. 2012. "Gendering the bricks and mortar: building an opportunity structure for equality bargaining". *Journal of Industrial Relations* 54(2), 147–63.

Williamson, S. & M. Baird 2014. "Gender equality bargaining: developing theory and practice". *Journal of Industrial Relations* 56(2), 155–69.

Wintour, N. 2011. "Achieving equality through quality: public services and the role of public sector trade unions". In V. Moghadam, S. Franzway & M. Fonow (eds), *Making Globalization Work for Women: The Role of Social Rights and Trade Union Leadership*. New York: SUNY Press.

Wintour, N. (ed.) 2012. Copa do Mundo para Todos: O Retrato dos Vendedores e Vendedoras Ambulantes nas Cidades-Sede Da Copa Do Mundo de 2014. Rio de Janeiro: Streetnet International.

Wintour, N. 2013. "Trends in freedom of association and collective bargaining since the 2008 financial crisis". Brussels: Education International. Available at: https://ei-ie.org/en/detail/2503/ei-releases-major-study-documenting-collective-bargaining-in-the-education-sector (accessed 8 September 2018).

Wintour, N. 2015. "Report on the quadrennial survey on equality and diversity, 2010–2014". Education International 7th World Congress. Congress proceedings, book #4B: quadrennial surveys. Brussels: Education International.

Withers, M. & J. Biyanwila 2014. "Patriarchy, labour markets and development: contesting the sexual division of labour in Sri Lanka". *IIM Kozhikode Society & Management Review* 3(1), 33–4.

Yeung, B. 2018. "How the most vulnerable workers are targeted for sexual abuse". *The Guardian*, 13 March. Available at: https://www.theguardian.com/news/2018/mar/13/how-the-most-vulnerable-workers-are-targeted-for-sexual-abuse (accessed 8 September 2018)

Zhang, T. *et al.* 2012. "An estimation of the economic impact of spousal violence in Canada, 2009". Ottawa: Department of Justice, Research and Statistics Division.

Index